GOT A LIGHT?

CONVERSATIONS WITH STRANGERS THAT SPARKED
MEANINGFUL CONNECTIONS & UNEXPECTED
REVELATIONS

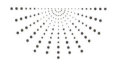

JASON FUERSTENBERG   MICHELLE SAVAGE

FRED SOUCIE   CHRISTY JAYNES   NATASHA CAMPISI

SHAY MICHELLE DRAPEAU   JENNIFER HURLEY

SUSIE MOCERI   NATASHA ZIKE

CONTENTS

SULIT PRESS

Ready to fast-track your publishing career, increase your visibility, or boost your business?

Harness the power of partnership by contributing a 3,000-word chapter to one of our upcoming Multi-Author Books!

If you are...
✅ Inspired by what you do and want to generously share what you've learned...
✅ Committed to meeting deadlines and doing your best work...
✅ Ready to connect with other aspiring authors who are as excited as you are to share your book with the world...
Then our Multi-Author Book might be the right path for you! Learn more at sulitpress.com/multi-author-books

1
EXORCISMS AND OTHER SIDE EFFECTS

JASON FUERSTENBERG

—————

The air in the dimly lit room was thick with tension and an overwhelming aroma of garlic and baked cheese. Food is a great way to break the awkwardness of an intervention, but I had no appetite.

"Manipulation, domination, and control," the man hovering above said to me. I was lying in bed, sweating profusely, refusing to eat the lasagna that he and his wife had prepared. "That's how the enemy got in, J."

The words hung between us, heavy and accusatory.

"It's witchcraft," he continued, his eyes locked onto mine, searching for signs of understanding or denial.

"Who am I manipulating?" I shot back, frustration in my

voice. "I pay for everyone, live in the garage downstairs, and don't ask anyone for anything."

"Not you," he replied, his tone softening yet resolute. "You're being manipulated, dominated, and controlled, and it has driven you crazy." There was a certainty in his voice, a spiritual diagnosis delivered with the precision of a practiced healer. Over time, I had learned confidence could cloak any statement in a veil of truth, compelling even the skeptics to listen.

"I need to cast these demons out of you," he said, his gaze filled with compassion as if he were offering a lifeline. Yet, beneath his kind eyes lay an indirect but clear accusation toward my wife.

I was nearing the end of the most difficult five-year period of my life. My wife, who was in the process of divorcing me, had arranged for this man to come and help me be "normal again." He had recently started a ministry focused on casting out demons and breaking chains of bondage in people's lives. She felt that calling in the exorcist would be my best shot at redemption—or possibly something that would look amazing in the divorce proceedings.

He placed his large sweaty hands on each side of my head as he started to thank God and began chanting in tongues. His forehead was scrunched up, and sweat formed. I couldn't help but stare at the drop of sweat running down each ridge of his forehead as he was at war with whatever demons he felt were controlling me.

At the time, I had no idea if some unholy force possessed me, but I did know my life was miserable, and any chance at feeling like myself again was worth a shot.

The last few years, I had been in and out of the psychiatrists' office, and the diagnoses and prescriptions kept changing. I went from being diagnosed as bipolar to not bipolar, then a "nonspecific personality disorder," and finally to good old-fashioned depression. With each diagnosis, the medication kept changing along with them. How much your life can change from a fifteen-minute doctor appointment is impressive.

He began to rock my head back and forth, chanting louder, and I started to feel my skin burning from head to toe.

"I have to go!" I yelled. "My skin is burning!"

"That's the demons, J. Let me finish praying!"

I snapped up from his holy grip, tears running down my face.

He was convinced a demon was manifesting from his prayers, but I knew what was really happening. I recalled reading the side effects of my latest medication:

a rash that escalates into head to toe blisters, suicidal thoughts, and a laundry list of other ailments.

I didn't have the heart to tell him.

I knew I had to get to the hospital fast. I ran down the apartment stairs, jumped on my bike, and rode to the hospital a few miles away.

What if my entire body turns into a blistering rash, I thought. *Great, this one is going to work against me in court.* The thoughts were running wind-sprints in my mind. *I am indeed a basket case.*

Life was pretty uncertain and lonely. I spent the last five years struggling and trying repeatedly to bring my life back from the dead. There are only so many times you can try to resurrect the dead, and I was driving myself insane in the process.

Although my wife never explicitly told me not to have family or friends, I could tell it was discouraged. She always had a reason why each person in my life was using me or taking advantage of me. She stayed home when I wanted to visit my family, and the kids were not allowed to go.

Over time, I isolated myself to the point of severe depression, and the few friends I did have I kept secret. If I went out with a friend or visited my family, I was accused of being selfish, taking time away from her and our blended family. As the sole provider, I knew that if I couldn't make the relationship work, I would lose not only everything, but everyone.

A common tactic of manipulation is often isolation. When you isolate yourself and shut your friends and family's voices out of your life, you only hear what is designed for you to hear. At a certain point, I gave up being myself and tried to be the person she needed me to be, and it had been slowly killing me for years. It felt like if I wanted to keep a relationship with my kids, I had to play by her rules.

Drippy Lip Lucy

"What brings you here tonight?" the hospital attendant asked.

"My skin feels like it's on fire!" I was sweating heavily and looked like a deranged lunatic.

"Are you on drugs, sir? List your medications on the form, please." She spoke in the most monotone voice I've ever heard. I scribbled the medication down—it was only one. She glanced at the form, talked to a coworker, and I was rushed to the secure ward of the hospital. An armed guard was stationed outside the room I was carted into. My phone was taken, my arms were strapped to the side of the hospital bed, an IV was administered, and minutes later, I passed out.

I woke up in an ambulance but couldn't say a word. Everything felt heavy; my eyelids felt weighted down, and I couldn't move a muscle. The ambulance stopped, and I was carted into another facility.

Where am I? I tried to say, but nothing came out.

This was my second 51/50 in the past year. The last visit was for shoving an entire bottle of antipsychotic medication down my throat. I was developing a reputation at the local hospital for being a risk, so they instantly sent me to the secure ward. A third visit would allow them to keep me involuntarily for several weeks.

They parked me in the hallway and waited for whatever drugs to wear off so I could speak. I was still secured to the gurney, and the fluorescent lights of the room were dancing misty circles in my mind. I could see mustard-yellow painted walls that were peeling and seemed to have some water damage, as there were darker brown water stains that looked to have run down the wall twenty years ago. The floors were a checkerboard linoleum tiling, faded and worn.

This place hasn't been updated since my birth, I thought, as I caught an avocado-green refrigerator out of the corner of my eye.

A short, tattooed man in hospital scrubs peered over me, speaking Spanglish.

"Sir, I need to inspect you for damage." I felt like a rental car being inspected for scratches and dents before driving it out of the parking lot. "What are these from?" he asked, pointing out the scrapes on the backs of my heels.

"I ride my bike a lot. I don't have a car," I answered with a slur.

He documented every scratch on my body, put down his clipboard, and turned to me. "Are you going to hurt yourself?"

"No sir."

He loosened my restraints, gave me a handful of pills, and escorted me to my room, a ten-foot by ten-foot space with six cots shared by both men and women deemed "not safe for society."

"I'm not gonna lie to you bro, it's tough to sleep in there. But I gave you something to knock you out," he said. I climbed into my cot on the top bunk, pulled the rough, scratchy brown wool blanket to my chin, and passed out instantly.

I woke up the following day feeling severely hungover. I'm not sure if it was from the old drugs wearing off or

the new handful of pills I got at bedtime. Crawling out
of bed, I wandered into the shared living space. Three
old brown upholstered couches sat in a U shape, which
pointed up at the television show "Rosanne" playing on
the wall mount TV. Various baked goods and cold coffee
were offered for breakfast.

"This coffee is cold," I said to the worker.

"We can't give you hot coffee. It's not safe to give unsafe
people something hot," he replied with an answer he
must have given hundreds of times before.

Sitting down with my cold bagel and cold coffee in the
living area, I looked around the room. Everyone was
watching TV except for one person. I watched this
young woman with curly, shoulder-length black hair
walking on a diagonal like in horror movies. I didn't
know walking with your head and shoulders so far in
front of your feet without falling over was possible. Her
skin was pale-looking and her eyes were lifeless. Drool
was falling down her outstretched lower lip as she
walked in circles around the couches. She seemed in a
hurry, but there was nowhere to go.

SLAM! She crashed her head into the glass door and
bounced off of it like a pinball, going the other direction
as if nothing had happened, leaving a drool print on the
glass.

"Who's that?" I asked the guy next to me on the couch.

"We call her Drippy Lip Lucy. She's been here awhile, longer than any of us," he said.

Another man playing checkers against himself let out a scream of terror and threw the board across the room, checkers flying past the TV screen. No one seemed surprised. Drippy Lip Lucy circled the couch repeatedly as we sipped our cold coffee, everyone acting like it was just another ordinary day at the asylum.

One of the psychiatric staff came in and called me for an assessment. We passed through the glass door, avoiding the drool imprint, and made our way into the examination room.

"I don't think I belong here. This shit is straight out of a movie."

"We have seventy-two hours to determine that, Jason," the doctor replied calmly.

"I need to leave," I insisted. "I run a business and people are counting on me. I did not ask for this."

"The hospital placed you on a psychiatric hold. You legally can't leave until you've been held for seventy-two hours. It's for your protection."

I sighed in frustration. I felt trapped, and everything was spiraling out of control.

The doctor continued. "Tell me Jason. I've been looking at your file. You've changed medication three times in the last three months, and your diagnosis keeps changing. What happened?"

The question hit me like a ton of bricks.

"I've been going through a divorce for a while now. I live in a garage beneath the apartment I pay for that the rest of my family lives in. I've lost my Jeep. It was repossessed. And I am about to be evicted from my apartment. Every area of my life is a literal dumpster fire. All I have left is my job, which I'm about to lose for being here."

There was a long pause as the doctor stared at his clipboard, seemingly unsure what to write. Finally, he looked up and said, "Jason, that's a lot to go through. What steps are you taking to cope with this loss and move on with your life?"

The fact was that I wasn't—coping, that is. I was holding on to a life that had rejected me, still hoping for some miraculous resurrection.

"Jason, what friends and family do you have in your life?"

wrongfully diagnosed and prescribed improper medication multiple times. In a different way, they told me what my exorcist friend had said: manipulation, domination, and control had influenced me to make all the wrong decisions for years.

"Jason, why aren't you doing the things that are important to you in your life? Nothing is holding you bac ᵢ right now. You should be focused on moving fo ward with your life."

7 he thought that had felt foreign was beginning to ound like an amazing idea. For over a decade, I had ɔeen conditioned to sacrifice myself for the greater good of my wife. If I moved on with my life, a part of me that I wanted so badly would be done for good. Struggling with mental health, the fear compounded.

"But...I don't even know who I am anymore." It was the lamest reply in the history of replies, but it was true.

The realization hit me—hard. All of this was my fault. No one made me do anything; it was ultimately my choice to isolate myself. It was my choice not to be myself. I couldn't blame anyone for that other than myself.

I was being released with a clean bill of mental health and left the clinic with only my phone, which the staff had so kindly charged, and a terrifying sense of starting over.

I took a deep breath as I stepped outside. The air felt different, fresher somehow as if signaling the start of a new chapter. My seventy-two hour stay had forced me to confront truths I had been avoiding for years: I was clinging to a life that had rejected me, hoping for a resurrection that would never come.

My journey of healing began when I realized that I had allowed manipulation and control to shape my identity. I was tired of being a character in someone else's story. I wanted to write my own.

Opening the Door

Determined to reclaim my life, I decided to do something that once felt unthinkable: I signed up for social media. You can't fill a need if you don't open a door to let it in. I knew I needed to have family back in my life. For years, I had shut myself off, closing the doors to the world to save my marriage. But now, as I stared at the screen, I realized it was time to bridge the gap I had created. Signing up for social media felt like the first step toward healing. I needed to reconnect, not just with the world, but with myself.

Opening these virtual doors wasn't just about no longer being alone, but about tearing down the walls I'd built around myself. I'd been playing a role for years, trying to be what I thought was needed. But now, it was time to see who would be interested in the real me. By putting myself out there, I was inviting others into my world, hoping to find genuine connections rather than the fake, forced ones I'd grown used to. When someone sees you for who you truly are and still wants you in their life, you know you are indeed worthy to them.

"I see you signed up for Facebook," a text message notification from my soon-to-be ex-wife popped up on my phone. Text bubbles appeared, then another message quickly followed: "I'm happy for you that you're moving on with someone else."

All the reasons I had been isolated came rushing back in. I had ten Facebook friends at this point, all family, and my wife already thinks I have a line of women in my DMs.

"Well, I guess I should be moving on too," she messaged again.

I couldn't fathom how having a presence in society and connecting with friends, family, and community was such a threat.

No reply! I thought, but my thumbs were already texting.

"I found out my grandfather is having his 101st birthday party and I'm going out of town to see him," I texted. It had been years and he was now into the triple digits. I had to go. I didn't care what the fallout was from her. I waited for the text bubbles or a reply but they didn't come.

My family welcomed me back with open arms, showing me that blood is thicker than water. They knew my struggles, and instead of judgment, I found support and understanding.

I got no "I told you so" or any type of guilt trip. My family had my back even though it seemed like I had turned my back on them. I felt supported and like an asshole at the same time.

The introverted Nomad

After returning to California, I bought an old van online and set to work, making it livable. I added a cot and a few milk crates for storage. I hung tropical print towels on the walls to give it personality and installed a color-changing light. It wasn't much, but it was my new home on wheels, which addressed two problems at once. I didn't have a car and I lost my garage living space after the eviction notice ran out.

I was paying for my ex's new apartment, and in California, it's tough to afford more than one place. Plus, my credit was now trashed. The only chance I had to make life work during this transition seemed to be van life. The idea of being on the hook for a second living space while struggling with mental health seemed like a recipe for disaster.

While traveling the country for work, I decided to post my photos of my travel adventures on social media. I made stops at interesting restaurants, coffee shops, and national parks, and shared these experiences online. I had previously traveled across the country during Covid but hadn't shared my journey publicly. Solo travel changes a lot when other people can join in on the experiences. It was a chance to inspire others, share beauty, offer something of value, and open myself to new connections and opportunities.

The people who embraced my weirdness and even encouraged it helped me on my journey to healing, accepting me for who I am and being okay with who I wasn't. By sharing my adventures, I was celebrating my new freedom and inviting others to participate. It felt like I was finally living for myself, allowing others to see the world through my eyes and maybe inspire them to embrace their uniqueness.

As I drove through the open landscape, I knew that the road ahead was full of possibilities. And for the first time in a long time, I felt at peace with where I was and excited about where I was going.

I started to see old friends and family begin to follow my posts. Some names I recognized, while others were a mystery. One name in particular stood out: Savage. I didn't know any Savages personally, but I knew it was my mom's maiden name. They had to be relatives, connected to me through her somehow.

Growing up, I lived with my dad and had never met any of my mom's side of the family other than her mom and that was once back in the eighties. The thought that I had a family I had never met sat in the back of my mind.

Eventually, I received a comment on one of my travel photos. "You certainly know how to live life, cuz!"

Cousin? I never considered that I might have a cousin I had not met. For some reason, my mom's side of the family always felt foreign and distant, like a different distant branch on the family tree. I picked up my phone.

"Mom, how am I related to Christy Savage?" I felt uncomfortable for not knowing the answer .

"Well, that's my older brother's daughter," she said.

I had never heard this name in my life. How could I go my entire lifetime and half my family are complete strangers? How many more family members have I never met before?

On one hand, I was losing my wife and the home life I fought so hard for. But on the other hand, I had half my bloodline waiting for me to meet them.

Intrigued, I reached out to Christy and we arranged to meet when I came to visit my grandfather for what would be his 102nd birthday. It had been quite the year.

During the sixteen-hour drive, with no music or podcasts, I felt a mix of excitement and anticipation buzzing through me like a pot of coffee on an empty stomach. Meeting people usually didn't faze me, but this was different. This was family. My mind raced through countless scenarios, imagining what it would be like to meet a stranger who shared my blood.

The Stories We Tell Ourselves

We are, each of us, a product of the stories we tell ourselves. - Derren Brown

Meeting Christy was like finding a missing piece of myself. Our connection was immediate, and our conversation flowed effortlessly. Her life was a shining example to living authentically and pursuing one's passions.

What was supposed to be a quick coffee turned into multiple coffees and then lunch, and before we knew it, hours had flown by.

"The way you live your life is so exciting and inspiring," she said, her eyes bright and piercing. "Look, you've designed a nomadic life, built a unique career, and love capturing it through photography. So many people would be interested in following along on your journey. It's a road hardly traveled."

I stared at my coffee, unsure of how to respond. I had always felt like I was living my plan b, a recovering train wreck still nursing the wounds of a life that had rejected me. Her words made me see my life through a different lens, one that was filled with possibility and resilience. The story I had been telling myself was drastically different and much more depressing.

"I went through a divorce, too, and met someone special after an ugly, difficult breakup. Now I'm married to a wonderful man who is supporting me making this move across the country, and I can't wait for him to join me here in St. Louis."

I had been going through a breakup for over half a decade at this point. My divorce paperwork got pushed back during Covid, and I've been legally separated and in the process of divorce for what felt like forever.

"I want to move on or receive some sort of miracle to fix everything," I said to her. "I love someone I wish I didn't, and I'm not sure how to handle that. I hate that I want to grow old with someone who makes me feel lost and alone. I can't picture having someone else to grow old with. We've had a family, been through tough times. And she's been my dream girl for nearly fifteen years."

Christy, a well-regarded life coach, listened intently. Her empathy and understanding provided a sense of comfort I hadn't felt in a long time. She was helping countless people recognize their life dreams and make them come true. It wasn't like she was pretending her life was perfect; she had faced difficulties as well and was making the best of things for her life. This wasn't token advice. I'm sure she made sacrifices for her new husband, but she was living life the way she designed, and he loved and supported her. This was the life example I needed.

I realized that I was building something new, something more permanent that could withstand the storms of life. Despite spending most of my time alone traveling, I could still have friends and family in my life. Opening the doors to communicate with strangers, checking in on friends and family, and not isolating myself needed to be pillars of my new foundation. She made me realize I had a different story to tell.

We said our goodbyes and vowed, like most do, to stay in touch. This felt real, however—not the mechanical pleasantries you say and don't mean.

If Christy hadn't reached out to me, I might have never met half of my family. I might have made that connection, but my doors were closed. I was too busy minding my business and avoiding communication. Isolation had led me to the clinic with Drippy Lip Lucy and countless wrong mental health diagnoses.

Christy saw in me a potential I had long forgotten about. Her words were healing to my soul, inspiring me to view my life through a lens of possibility rather than defeat.

I realized I had been telling myself the wrong story. Instead of being a victim of circumstance, I could be the hero of my narrative. My journey was one of rebuilding —creating a life that could withstand the storms I had weathered. The nomadic life I led was not a plan b; it was an opportunity to redefine myself on my terms.

As I drove away from St. Louis, I reflected on my conversation with Christy. I understood my life was not about returning to the past or clinging to old dreams. It was about embracing the present and the future with open arms. It was about allowing myself to be vulnerable, to connect with others, and to live authentically.

With each mile, I felt the desperation to resurrect my failed life lift. Sometimes, our best life happens through failure.

I was living a life I had designed, filled with genuine connections and experiences. I had learned that being true to myself was the key to unlocking life's richness. By letting people in, I avoid loneliness and embrace the strength of shared experiences and mutual support.

On the road, I realized that I didn't have to have all the answers. Life was about embracing the journey, not necessarily knowing the destination.

The story I told myself was now quite different, and I would not have realized this without that conversation I had with my long-lost cousin.

From that day forward, a lot in my life changed. There is power in owning who you are and embracing it. Moving from self-loathing to acceptance, and ultimately becoming my own best friend, was one of the most powerful experiences of my life. I became much more open to meeting people, connecting with family, and taking on fun new experiences.

Shortly after, I connected with Christy's younger sister, Michelle, on Facebook. They were releasing a multi-author book called *Show Your Work* and had opened sign-ups for their next project, which was focused on travel.

I thought to myself, I wish I could write—that would be a cool way to support my cousins and go through the experience together. I really couldn't imagine a better way to get to know each other.

I felt like my lifestyle was a perfect match for the story, but I wasn't sure if I could put my experiences into words. I hadn't written anything since high school, and quite frankly, I barely made it out with a diploma.

A few weeks after the project had already started, I decided to join in. *Better late than never,* I thought, even though my lack of experience made me worry I'd either be a burden or make a massive fool of myself.

I ended up telling the story of my travels for work during Covid across the country. When launch day came for the book, I was absolutely shocked—not only was I now a published author, but the book hit bestseller status in multiple categories, and an excerpt of my story was even shared in USA Today!

To celebrate, a book signing party was announced in Austin, TX. I loaded up the van again, with the anxious anticipation of meeting more of the family tree for the first time.

Not long ago, I walked out of a faded psychiatric clinic, the kind of place where hope feels as worn as the linoleum floors. Released from a 51/50 hold, carrying the weight of uncertainty on my shoulders.

Back then, the future was a blur, something I couldn't quite grasp. But as I stood there surrounded by new family and friends, I realized I wasn't just celebrating the release of a book—I was celebrating the return to a life I never thought possible. A life that was no longer defined by fear or the echoes of past mistakes.

This journey showed me our darkest moments aren't the end of the story; they're the cracks where the light gets in. This was a celebration of a new life, free from exorcisms and other side effects.

JASON FUERSTENBERG

Jason Fuerstenberg is an Amazon bestselling author and photographer while still maintaining his day job traveling nomadically for his clients in the coffee industry.

He is currently working on his first solo writing project, tackling the tough topic of self-destructive personalities in a shocking memoir. The story shared in *Got a Light?* is a portion of this exciting new project.

The best place to keep in touch is on instagram @driftlessone

2

REDEMPTION

MICHELLE SAVAGE

⬤▬▬▬

*a*s a newly minted member of TSA's pre-check status, I still arrived too early for my flights. Instead of waiting in the security line for two hours like a commoner, I waited at my gate for two hours like someone with new money, not yet accustomed to the luxury of leaving my shoes on through security. I suppose sitting at the gate was preferable to standing in line, so at the very least, I'd upgraded the quality of my waiting.

With ample time before boarding my flight to Phoenix, I wandered through the Austin airport, pondering how a day can start so pleasant and instantly take a turn for the worst. At least in the movies, you get a heads-up with some ominous music or the eerie echo of a cawing bird. (By the way, I looked up what kind of bird makes the scary sound in horror movies, and it is called a common loon, which is really just saying the bird is basic and crazy.) The point I was groping for was that real life is nothing like the movies. Sometimes, with no warning at all, the universe would back up and take an astral crap on your life.

Just hours earlier, I'd set out to grab a smoothie and soak up some sun before my flight. I'd been anticipating this trip for weeks, especially since my client booked me a room in a swanky hotel while we worked through the final edits of her book. It would practically feel like a vacation. Then, backing out of my driveway, I noticed I missed a call and recognized the number was from my son's school.

"Hello, this is Mrs. Savage, Joaquin's mom. I just missed your call. Is everything okay?"

"Well, no. We have Joaquin here in the nurse's office. He got into a fight and his hand looks pretty injured. It appears both boys are at fault and had planned the fight out in advance. Are you able to come pick him up?"

"Are you kidding me? I can NOT believe he would get into a fight, especially at school. And they planned it?!"

"Your son says he fought the other boy because he had been bullying a kid with special needs and he was also talking inappropriately about your son's girlfriend."

Oh wonderful, I thought, *I've raised a vigilante.*

Cradling his swollen hand on a bag of ice, my son looked like a whipped puppy on the drive home.

"I'm so sorry, Mom. Mom! Mom, I know I messed up. I'm so sorry."

I was a dozen clicks beyond yelling and the only words I could utter came out slowly in a deep tone that sounded like I was possessed.

"Joaquin, your words don't mean shit to me right now. You were supposed to be rebuilding my trust after the stunt you pulled *last* week, and *this* is what you do? It doesn't matter whether or not the other kid had it coming. You are not the fist of karma!"

I could feel him staring at me, waiting for a reassuring look to let him know I still loved him and everything would be okay, but I refused to cave. He needed to know I'd hit my limit. While this fight was his first, it was not a solo incident of bad behavior. Just a week earlier, he and two of his buddies dressed up in Spider-man costumes and started a bonfire in a public park at 3 a.m. When a neighbor woke up to see flames behind his house, he called the fire department, which automatically summoned the police. My dear boy and his crime-fighting friends spent the rest of the night hiding from the authorities until they escaped to the friend's house where they were supposed to be sleeping.

The appointment for my son to get his hand X-rayed wasn't until 7 p.m. and someone else would be taking him to the doctor. I felt guilty for not being there. I had cared for my son through every bump and bruise for all of his fourteen years, but now, I'd be 30,000 feet in the air by the time he'd find out if his hand was broken. I wished I could skip ahead to the day we could look back and say, "I'm so grateful this all happened because look at all the wonderful things that came out of it." Even though I know, with my whole heart, this is how the universe works—that our good is coming to us all the time even when it looks like everything is falling apart—I was too mired in the suck to feel optimistic.

After ordering some tacos for my dinnertime flight, I headed to my gate where there were two open seats left, one next to a mom with a flailing toddler and the other next to a guy wearing a maroon sweatsuit and socks with what looked like government sandals. After a quick deliberation, I decided I'd rather sit by the cagey-looking sweatsuit guy with neck tattoos, wagering he'd be less inclined to strike up any small talk. I fucking hate small talk, but hate it even more when I'm stressed.

Slumping into my seat, I looked on as a tall, red-faced man in a purple bowler's hat imposed himself on anyone who would listen. His first victims were a young college-aged couple.

"Hey! You're going to Phoenix too?" he bellowed.

They smiled politely and brushed him off, pretending to be engrossed in whatever was playing on their iPad. Undeterred, the man sought out more strangers with whom he wanted to engage. I focused on the tacos in my lap, deliberately avoiding eye contact. I was already all amped up with nowhere to go, and the last thing I needed was to be accosted by some over-eager traveler.

Who knew what inspired me to do this, but after staring blankly into my food, I turned toward sweatsuit guy and said, "Excuse me, but would you like one of my tacos? I can't eat them both and I'd hate for one to go to waste."

Nodding briefly in my direction, he said, "Yes, ma'am. Thank you, ma'am. I appreciate it, ma'am."

Using my lid as a second plate, I handed him my other brisket taco and wondered if sharing tacos now meant we were obliged to speak to one another.

"Wow, these are pretty good," I said. "I didn't even realize how hungry I was."

"Yes ma'am," he agreed. "Thank you so much."

"Please stop calling me ma'am. It makes me feel old," I smiled.

He asked me, "What are you going to Phoenix for? Is that where you live?"

"No, I live here. I'm just flying out there for work. How about you?"

"I just got out of prison today and I'm flying home to get a job and take care of my mom."

"You got out today?! Oh, wow! This is a big day for you. How long were you in prison?"

"Well, I went in when I was fourteen, and I'm about to turn thirty-eight so I guess it's been twenty-four years."

Now, mind you, if someone goes to prison for twenty-four years when they are only fourteen, it is not because they got caught skipping school or stealing candy from the grocery store. Only murder or some other heinous crime that also includes murder awards you that kind of sentence. Knowing this, I decided not to ask what he'd been in for.

He motioned to the people waiting who were on their phones and noted, "When I went to prison, we still used a phone that was connected to the wall, and now everyone carries around a phone that's like a little computer."

I thought of how untethered he must feel, going from the confines and structure of prison to an airport. All that open space. All those people he didn't know. He had no luggage to carry on, and I wondered if he had any money on him at all. He seemed simultaneously like a scared child, daunted by his inexperience in the modern world, and like a wild animal, made fierce from the hard work of surviving.

But when you meet someone like sweatsuit guy, covered in crudely drawn, hand-poked tattoos, it's hard not to feel a sense of compassion and sadness that so many prime years of his life had already been lost.

My son was only fourteen. Just a boy, really. A good kid with a big brain and a kind heart, but he was already making mistakes despite having guidance and support. Just imagine if he didn't have that. Perhaps realizing sweatsuit guy went to prison at my son's age is what drew out my maternal instincts. It's not like this guy needed to be saved by a middle-class, mom-crusader, but he could do with some respect and maybe a friend.

Warming to him, I said, "I guess I should tell you congratulations? Or maybe it's better to say 'Happy Birthday' since this is the first day of your new life."

He cracked the faintest smile, and I hoped he could sense even a glimmer of possibility for himself.

But his half-smile disappeared as his eyes darted nervously around the room, "What time do we get on the plane?"

I looked at the reader board and said, "It looks like the flight is delayed by a few minutes. You see there?" I pointed. He nodded and clutched his paper ticket. The taco had made me thirsty, and I sipped my water, wondering if he was thirsty, too.

The red-faced man grew increasingly unhinged. Approaching a crowd of travelers forming nearby, he shouted, "Do you want me to leave you alone? My dad just got cancer and today I lost my job!"

Sweatsuit guy nodded in the direction of red-faced man and said, "One thing I learned in prison is how to spot the crazies from a mile away."

I laughed, "Yeah, I can't tell if that guy took something he shouldn't have or didn't take something that he needs. Thank God this flight has open seating, so you can avoid sitting next to him!"

"Open seating?" He looked confused.

Oh right, this guy has probably never been on an airplane before.

"It means you can choose any seat you want, but you have to board with your group. Can I see your ticket?"

He handed me his crumpled paper ticket. and I showed him that he was in group C and pointed to the pillar where he would line up when his group was called. After twenty-three years in prison, he was probably used to lining up and being called out by a number. At least now, it was by choice.

On the sly, I texted my client in Phoenix, who is a counselor and has contacts with many nonprofits in the area, and asked if I could give her number to a guy who'd just gotten out of prison. (This illustrates the downside of being my friend.) With her consent, I jotted her number on a napkin and gave it to him.

"If you need a job or anything else, this person might be able to help you."

When my group was called to board, I said goodbye to sweatsuit guy and wished him luck.

I took a seat in the aisle, hoping I'd be able to sleep, but as a rookie to frequent travel, I stupidly picked a seat in front of the exit row, which meant my seat wouldn't recline.

After distracting myself with the finale episode of the reality show I'd downloaded to my phone, I closed my eyes and took a nose-dive into self-pity, remembering how challenging the past few years had been. What with parenting through a pandemic and my son's failing grades, and his father moving away and now this bout of vandalism and violence. As both good cop and bad cop, I was already using all the parenting tools I had, which left me exhausted and terrified that no matter how hard I tried or how much I loved him, I would ultimately fail him. This last thought filled my eyes with tears and I breathed deeply to compose myself.

Don't cry, don't cry, don't cry. But whatever pins had been holding me together were suddenly plucked away and I began to sob. Using my scarf to mop away snot and tears, I was relieved the plane's cabin was dark, except for a few reading lights.

"Are you okay?" asked the young woman sitting beside me.

Inhaling deeply and wiping my eyes again, I sniffed and sighed, "Yes, I'm fine. It's just been a tough day."

"I've had a really hard day, too," she said.

"I'm sorry to hear that," I replied, but I couldn't decide if it was polite for her to commiserate or rude to turn the topic toward herself when my suffering was obviously greater.

As if she hadn't just witnessed me ugly crying in public, she whispered, "I've wanted to ask you this for the whole flight but didn't want to seem weird. Can I read your palm? I've been practicing for a few months now."

"Um, sure. As long as my palm doesn't tell you I die in a plane crash. That would be bad news for both of us."

Hovering the flashlight from her phone over my palm, she pointed to the bump on my thumb and said, "See how your thumb joint juts out right here? That says you're very independent. You like working for yourself or being your own boss."

"Uh-huh," I nodded along, "That's for sure!"

"This line here is bumpy, which tells me you're very passionate and put all of yourself into everything you do, whether it's work or relationships."

Man, she's good!

"And this is your relationship line. Hmmm, have you been married before?"

"Yes, I was married to my son's father a long time ago, but I've been with my current husband for eleven years."

"The marriage you are in is a strong relationship and is a good partnership for you. Also, your lifeline is long."

(Now that I'm divorced for a second time, I'll chalk up that last part to her inexperience.)

Who was to say if this amateur palm reader really believed what she was telling me or if she was just trying to cheer me up, but her affirmations about how awesome I was instantly pulled me out of my abyss and halted my unraveling. If words really did have power, this was direct evidence.

Somebody once told me about an experiment where, if you said mean things to a container of water, froze that water, and then examined it under a microscope, the water crystals would appear in ugly, jagged, irregular patterns. But, if you spoke kindly to the water before freezing it, the pattern would be as lovely and beautiful as a snowflake. Perhaps the coolest thing about water was that even if it was frozen for ten thousand years, it could still be melted and reshaped, over and over again, forever. It held the very essence of redemption and transformation and lucky for us, it made up 80% of who we are.

I wondered what story the palm reader would decipher from the lines on sweatsuit guy's hands. Was there a line that diverged into separate branches, as if he'd had a choice to take a different path when he was younger? Or did the line swerve early on, only to straighten out later? Maybe his life was predestined to turn out exactly like it had, but I couldn't help but wonder what would have happened if someone had spoken life into him when he was a boy. Would a more pleasant arrangement of his crystals have prevented him from committing a crime in the first place?

Being told about my attributes did more than distract me from my meltdown or stroke my ego; it helped transform the jagged parts of me that had frozen under the pressure of fear, self-doubt, and anger. How different might life have been if everyone used their words to heal and create rather than to degrade and destroy? What if I spent less time chastising my son for his failing grades, threatening consequences, or dangling my lost trust in front of his face and spent more time reminding him how genuinely incredible he is? It seemed it could only arouse positive aspects in him and improve his chances for happiness and success. At the very least, it would strengthen our relationship, which would certainly impact my life for the better.

I couldn't read palms and, unless I buy a crystal ball or adopt a common loon as my next pet, I'd likely have more days that snuck up behind me and knocked me down without warning. Hopefully, the next time it happened I could skip the drama and jump right to the part where I was grateful for whatever good things would come from the situation because I already knew, without a doubt, that this was always true.

MICHELLE SAVAGE

Michelle Savage is an international best-selling author, keynote speaker, and the founder of Sulit Press, a boutique, non-fiction publishing house based in Austin.

Michelle has helped dozens of entrepreneurs, executives and visionaries become bestselling authors in half the time it takes to go it alone - while ensuring exceptional quality and results.

With philanthropy and social impact as a cornerstone of her company, Michelle is proud to donate all proceeds from Sulit's multi-author books to non-profits benefiting children in her community.

She believes everyone has a story worth telling and is passionate about helping them tell it well.

Website: www.sulitpress.com
Instagram: https://www.instagram.com/sulitpressbooks/
Facebook: https://www.facebook.com/SulitPress
LinkedIn: https://www.linkedin.com/in/michelle-savage-43032659/

3

MY FIERCE, IRISH LIGHT

FRED SOUCIE

I know Annie is dying now. That is why I am here. To walk with her for a bit along the sacred path of dying. I do not want Annie to be alone when she dies. I am here to love this woman who has brought such light into my life during some of my darkest days.

I am sitting in a padded fold-up chair next to her hospital bed in a hospice center in St. Paul where Annie has been brought to take her last breath.

The doctors say Annie is comatose. I don't know comatose, but I know Annie is unconscious, lying on her back, the head of the bed slightly raised. Her jaw muscles are done with their life of work, her mouth is agape.

The room is painted light green and wallpaper strips full of beautiful flowers that outline the top of each wall. Pleasant. A lot of work has been done to make this room pleasant.

Annie is in a hospital gown with a sheet covering her up to her chest. It is early evening and a cold winter day. The overhead lights have been dimmed.

Why do I want to be with this magnificent woman in her moment of death? Because I do. I just do. Annie is in her late seventies. She is my best friend and has been the biggest fan I have ever had in my years on earth. We have been on so many adventures where we shared our hearts. Annie is a passionate Irish woman, and when she loves you, it is with a fierceness beyond compare.

I begin a forced one-way conversation. "Annie, remember when you and I started the riot at the St. John's versus St. Thomas basketball game? Well, YOU really started it. Thank God we did not get maced or arrested in the middle of that, right?"

"So, Annie, you always want to know about my little brothers. Hal is a painter here in Minnesota. Ray Is back living in Illinois with Mom."

I tell Annie about many things in my life. Clumsy at first. What am I gonna talk about with this dying best friend?

After several hours Annie's hospice nurse checks her over. "Fred, Annie is dying but it could be a matter of hours, probably at least a few. She is going to die though, either tonight or within the next day. Two at the absolute most. You look like you could use some rest."

"May I please give you my cell number and could you call me if there's any change?" I say.

"Well yes, of course. I also have Father Lavin's phone number at St. Thomas. He also wants me to call if there's any change so he can give Annie the last rites," she says.

"If ever a saint has walked the face of the Earth, it is Father James Lavin," I reply. While I need rest, I want to be with her when she departs this earthly realm. I have no idea about whether Annie is aware of me, feeling my presence, or hearing a darn thing I say to her but with my tears there is also joy in reliving some of our great adventures together. How fitting that our unusual, warm, and comforting kinship begins and ends in the cold, sterile environment of a hospital room. As I sit on death watch for Annie, I can't help but think of the first time I met her.

* * *

Boy was I nervous. I could feel a huge knot in my belly and sweat trickling down my spine as I sat in the reception room of the college infirmary, waiting with the other muscle-bound guys to be called to see the campus doctor, Dr. Fox, so he could clear me to play my first season of football at the College of St. Thomas in St. Paul, Minnesota.

I was amongst total strangers and egos that ran rampant in this part of college life. Away from my hometown Elgin, Illinois for the first time, hoping—no, *needing*-- desperately to be a college football star like I was a star at St. Edward Central Catholic High School.

This was high stakes for me.

I was all-conference in our strong, suburban Chicago catholic conference. I was also all-Chicago area, according to the Chicago Sun Times. But I didn't feel like a star in that moment.

The infirmary consisted of the reception/waiting room, where we sat with a dozen red vinyl-covered stainless steel framed chairs and a steel desk for the college nurse. There was also an examination room right behind the desk, the nurse's quarters, a kitchen, and two patient rooms with hospital beds.

Sitting there in the waiting room, I was a boy afraid. Afraid of not making the team. Afraid of not making the grade in college. Afraid of flunking out. My mother told me earlier that spring that she had been told by my teachers I was not "college material." And perhaps, my mother suggested, I should attend the junior college in Elgin instead of St. Thomas. What a great confidence builder.

I was afraid of not making any friends. I was especially afraid of not having enough money. I was afraid of not fitting in. More than that, I was afraid of being a big, fat failure.

Where the fuck does all this come from? I mean, come on. I was senior class president, honor society, captain of the football team and the track team, and I worked during school to pay my own tuition. I was even voted homecoming king, for cripes sake. How elegant I looked sitting on the throne next to my drop-dead gorgeous queen and girlfriend, Judy McConaughey, an Irish lass with raven black hair and incredible blue eyes that melted my heart. She sat with her hand on mine in the newspaper photo that covered the entire front page of the *Elgin Free Press,* which was delivered to every door in Elgin.

A wonderful matriarch of thirteen children, Mrs. "Ma" Flood, whom I grew to love over time, told me years later, "Freddy, you were that cocky kid from Chicago who blew into town and took the campus by storm!"

Well, I felt anything but cocky sitting in the reception room on that ninety-five-degree sweltering day. The truth was I was a boy with a broken heart.

During my junior year in high school, my father decided to jump ship and abandon Mom and the five of us kids still living at home, of which I was the oldest.

One night my father did not come home. He never came home again.

I was crushed. I could not feel the firmament under my feet. I felt a white-hot poker in my belly as my world came crashing down around me. What was wrong with me that would cause my dad to abandon me like this?

On top of the shock of Dad bailing out, in the following months, I was thrust by my mother into the role of substitute/surrogate father to my four younger siblings. Talk about being set up to fail. How is any seventeen-year-old kid going to pull that off? I tried my best but my whole life I have felt I did not do a good enough job.

It turned out Dad left us for a much younger woman who just happened to work for him in his jewelry store business. My mother was devastated. Her hurt came out as fury. No, dark unrelenting rage at my father. So while she may have been screaming about my father, she was in *my* face screaming her rage at *me*. Literally in my face.

I could not hate my mother. Just could not. But a fire of hate grew in my belly at my father. There was no other place to put it. *I love you Daddy, but I hate your fucking guts for abandoning me, sticking me with to trying to play father to your other children and incur my mother's wrath with dirt for child support on top of it all.* This was a terrible time for me. I was forced into this trap to hate my father in order to survive the insanity of my scorned mother. But at the same time, I loved my daddy and so longed for his approval.

I had been knocking myself out to gain his approval for years. When I was little, my dad was a great, hands on, goofy and loving father. Usher in church, Boy Scout leader, he had a great job as the Dean of the Elgin National Watch Company, which trained people to become watch-makers; the old wind-up watches that most people reading this will not remember.

This prestigious watch company got knocked on its ass when the Swiss developed the dirt-cheap watch "movement" that allowed them to make inexpensive watches and put Elgin Watches out of business.

My father decided to open a jewelry store. He had charisma and was quite gregarious, but he struggled to be successful. Some of us are just not meant to be entrepreneurs. Dad treated his struggle to be successful and other problems with alcohol.

God only knows how my life would have turned out had my father not been forced into his new venture.

The stakes were high as I sat in that infirmary surrounded by older, bigger, and more talented men. *I cannot fail. I must not fail. I have to succeed. Have to.*

A woman, the nurse, was sitting at a steel desk in front of the door to the examination room. She was about sixty years old or so. She was almost as big around as she was tall, with short gray/white hair that looked like she just pushed back with her hands, instead of using a brush or comb. She wore a crisp white coat, fairly thick glasses, and had a low gravelly voice. Looking down at her list of players, she furrowed her brow and called out, "*Soo Chee?*"

There was an intensity, a fierceness about her, maybe even an ornery quality. She looked to be serious, all business. Her name was Anne Scanlan. But, "Don't you call me Anne!" It's "Annie," if you know what's good for you.

Irish. Boisterous. Ornery.

I walked over to her desk and said, "Hello. It's actually pronounced Soo see."

Handing me a glass urine specimen bottle she said, "Here, go down the hall and drink a toast to the governor...SOO CHEE," louder than the first time she mispronounced by name, a cantankerous look on her face.

A little taken a back, I took the specimen bottle from her and found myself chuckling on the way to the men's room where I laughed so hard, it was a challenge for me to hit the target. My nervousness dissolved into thin air. It is hard to be anxious and tense when you are laughing.

Little did I know that day how much of my freshman year would be spent in one of those hospital beds under Annie's watchful eye. A short couple of weeks later, I ended up in one of the infirmary beds with torn ligaments in my lower leg because of an illegal block, called a "clip," by a rascal of a player from St. Norberd's College. *Fuck, does that hurt!* I couldn't step on my left foot without a lot of pain. Dr. Fox taped it up, gave me a pair of crutches and moved me into the infirmary for a couple of days. This was the first of many infirmary stays that year.

Midwinter, I fractured my thumb on Tom Beranek's head with a helluva right hook. Unfortunately for me, only my thumb connected. I could actually hear the bone break on contact. We were sparring in preparation for the St. Thomas Silver Gloves tournament, with only a few days to go before the bouts began. The tournament was a big deal and I was crestfallen that I fractured my thumb.

My father taught me to box when I was around five or six. My brother Les, one year my senior (to the day), was my most frequent practice partner. We got along great, except when we didn't. Man, could we fight. Dad was a boxer in the Navy during World War II. Whenever we would start to scrap, Dad made us put on his old boxing gloves—which reached all the way to our elbows. "Now, you two are going to fight like men." He would referee the fights in our living room.

I wanted so badly to be a Silver Gloves champion during my freshmen year. *Then, I know I will count for something. Right?* I trained hard. Really hard. I ran. I lifted weights. I hit the punching bag. I sparred every day. *I am going to win.*

At the hospital after that fateful right hook, my injury required surgical repair and an "ex-fix," meaning the surgeon left a metal pin protruding from my thumb, with traction bands attached to a metal brace sticking out of a plaster cast. It was grotesque, to put it mildly.

"Dr. Fox can we please just wrap my fixed hand in a bunch of foam?" I asked. "I can box one-handed. I will still win," I was dead-serious. I was also nuts. I am right-handed. The fracture was to my right thumb.

Dr. Fox emphatically said, "No way."

On the night of the championship, which I could only attend as a spectator, I attended a "river party" on the banks of the Mississippi River a few blocks from campus after the bouts. In attendance were "Tommies" from the College of St. Thomas' all-male campus, and "Katies," our female counterparts from the College of St. Catherine. Fueled by alcohol (only my second time drinking that year), I leap up from my seat in the sand to chant,

"Fred be nimble,

Fred be quick!

Fred jump over the bonfire!"

And, I did. After escaping those leaps unscathed, I somehow ended up on the campus of Macalester College, one of our neighboring schools about a mile down the road. Young, dumb, and drunk, I started yelling "Tackle by Soucie," as I ran down a small tree or other object, tackling imaginary ball carriers. On one such tackle, I landed wrong and separated my shoulder.

Just like the fractured thumb, this landed me in the hospital for a few days, after which I graduated into the infirmary for a while. My right hand was in a big awkward cast and my left arm was in a sling.

Annie, for all her bluster and cantankerousness, had a caring heart. She was just what the doctor ordered for lightening my heavy heart and for lighting up my spirit through all that darkness. She had a knack for taking me outside of my worry.

"What are you going to break next Soo Chee? Huh?"

"I don't know, Annie?" I would reply. "What should I break next?"

Gruff, boisterous Annie Scanlan had a great sense of humor underneath her grumpy countenance. We would laugh together but we also talked about life. From Annie, I learned a lot about how to listen to other people, and really tune in. By the end of that year, I felt her strong love. She simply loved me through all of the problems I faced.

Annie became my best friend and, dare I say, I became her best friend that year as well. An eighteen-year-old college kid and a sixty-plus-year-old college nurse with a tough façade and a loving heart.

We often ate together in the cafeteria. I rarely drank during my college years, but I would sometimes buy a six-pack of beer through an older student and stop by the infirmary in the evening to visit while she was on duty. Annie would drink the six-pack in about an hour and a half while we talked and watched TV.

Annie was a St. Thomas athletics superfan. She had a rawhide rope with a bunch of cowbells attached that she brought to every single football and basketball game. I loved hearing her cow bells clambering and clattering from the stands and Annie's booming voice echoing throughout the stadium "Kill 'em Soo Chee!" She never did pronounce my name right, which was, and still is, a treasure to me.

Annie and I always sat together at St. Thomas basketball games and I'd always buy us each a Coke. Annie would drink hers halfway down, sometimes more, and surreptitiously open her purse and pour her hidden half pint of Irish whiskey, making her Coke bottle full again.

Our fiercest basketball rivalry was against St. John's University in Collegeville, Minnesota. The gymnasium was always filled to and beyond capacity at either school for these faceoffs. One winter night my senior year, Annie and I were at St. John's. The place was packed, not an empty seat in the house and some standing. Under one basket the bleachers were crammed with many rowdy (drunk) St. John's fans. The opposite end of the court was filled with many rambunctious (drunk) St. Thomas fans. Annie and I were sitting on the first row of bleachers. It was hard for her to climb any higher. She was really rocking it with her cowbells.

During a time-out, a St. John's fan, at least half drunk, walked directly in front of all of us and gave us all the finger. He slowly walked from our right side to our left side with a "fuck you" look on his face. If he knew Annie Scanlan, he would never have behaved so foolishly. When he was directly in front of us, Annie swung her bells and smacked him right in the butt.

The guy turned around with his fist cocked to hit Annie. Well, that sure wasn't going to happen. I stood up and dropped him and all hell broke loose. The St. John's fans at the other end of the court emptied the stands and rushed across the floor, probably to kill me, but then the St. Thomas fans erupted onto the court. We had a full-fledged riot on our hands. Thank you, Dad, for teaching me how to box.

I have vivid memories of that riot. Two St. John's fans attacked me. One jumped on my back, while the other punched me in my face. Somehow, I ended up flipping the guy on my back onto the floor. I was on top of him while his friend kept punching me in the head from behind. In the middle of this riot, I heard Annie's voice, "You leave Soo Chee alone! You leave Soo Chee alone!" as she hit the guy slugging me.

God bless you, Annie.

I was amazed to see her in the middle of the fray defending *me*. I should not have been, however. Annie had been a front-line Army nurse in the European Theatre during WWII. Fierce. Ornery. *Loving*. Annie.

The other vivid memory I have of that night is a really big state trooper with his forearm against my throat pinning me against the wall and calmly saying, "Settle down now, settle down now," over and over again. It finally sank in for me and I said, "Yes sir. Yes sir." and probably repeated it ten times. I raised both of my hands in surrender and felt him let up on the pressure when he could tell I was done.

Annie and I grew closer over my years at St. Thomas. Annie had strong opinions about right and wrong and she was right about them. Neither Annie nor I could stand bullies of any ilk. She had no reservations about getting in the face of some jock or fraternity guy picking on those "beneath them."

One evening, in line for dinner at the college cafeteria, Annie and I were in line to eat when Annie saw one of our special students (who today, we would probably say was on the spectrum) being picked on. "SOO CHEE, come with me!" she commanded. Together we walked up to the place in the line where these guys were picking on a guy we should all be helping rather than harassing.

"You leave Bob alone. Who gave you the crown to be above any of the rest of us?!" Annie declared. I was very happy to be by her side when she did things like this. I think Annie and I must've been illegitimate twins separated at birth when these kinds of things came up. She knew she could count on me to help her in any way I possibly could for anything whatsoever. (Though we never robbed a bank or anything like that.)

On the night of the collegiate Silver Gloves boxing tournament on campus my sophomore year, Annie was entertaining friends who drove up from Chicago to watch the fight and stopped by the infirmary to visit. I was fighting light heavyweight that night which was the second to last bout of the evening. I was too nervous to hang out around the locker room or in the armory where the crowd was going crazy so I took a walk and quite naturally ended up in the infirmary to visit with Annie.

These two fellows were sitting in the reception area when I walked in and Annie introduced them to me and then said she needed to go check on a student back in one of the rooms.

I had trained like a fiend to get ready for this. Our best boxer on campus was a fellow named Phil Huyer from the Bahamas. I think he was also the best athlete of any of us at Saint Thomas. He was an all-American sprinter, a fantastic soccer player, one hell of a good man and he was undefeated in the Silver Gloves championship. That year he decided to move from up the 165 pound "middleweight" class to my 175 pound "light heavyweight" class. No one else registered in his weight class. Everybody knew how good Huyler was. No one could possibly beat him.

Annie's two visitors were telling me that they drove all the way up from Chicago to watch Phil Huyler fight. He was the best boxer they had ever seen, even better than the pros on TV. "I feel sorry for the guy that's gotta fight Phil Huyler tonight."

The other fellow chimes in "Yep, that guy ain't got no chance against Huyler. He's gonna get killed."

I shared with them "Phil is the best boxer I have ever seen also. His opponent is gonna have one hell of a fight on his hands."

Annie came out from the patient room and into the lobby and said, "SOO CHEE is gonna fight tonight!"

One of the young men looked at me and said, "Oh yeah? Who are you gonna fight?"

I quietly said, "Phil Huyler."

Annie's friend laughed and mockingly said, "Good luck with that!"

(I have to confess Annie has truly amazed me at different times and this is one of them.) With no warning or hesitation whatsoever she hauled back and hit this guy so hard on the shoulder she knocked him off his chair. Standing over him, she shouted, "SOO CHEE is going to WIN!"

This guy must have loved Annie at least half as much as me because he wasn't mad at all. He got up and shrugged his shoulders and said "sorry Annie but …."

I left about then to go down to the armory and get my hands wrapped and otherwise prepare for this impossible fight. "God bless you, Annie Scanlon! " I said along the way.

Of course, Annie was in the first row of spectators in the aisle where fighters enter the ring. She hugged me just before I climbed into the ring and forcefully said, "Kill him SOO CHEE!" She was also the first one to give me a congratulatory hug just after I stepped out of the ring. Oh, what joy to be a friend of Annie Scanlon's.

Years later, when Annie hung up her stethoscope, I organized a retirement dinner for her on campus. The dining room was packed. People came from all over the United States—and two from Europe—to honor this remarkable woman.

I started my tribute to Annie, "What a gift to all of us Annie has been over so many years..." After my speech, I presented Annie with a large silver chalice engraved with a message of love and appreciation.

After the dinner, Annie said, "Let's go to Mitch's bar," a St Paul institution on West 7th Avenue. Chuck Mitch was a hell of a guy who also loved Annie. He continued refilling her brand-new silver chalice with beer the entire night. What an honor to drink from the same cup as Annie.

* * *

The fighting is done now for Annie. I don't want to leave her, but I am bone-tired and Annie probably isn't even aware I am here anyway. I lean over Annie's bed to kiss her goodbye. I kiss her forehead and then lightly kiss her lips. When I do she kisses me back...firm kiss, lips closed. I feel the hair on the back of my neck stand straight out and a lightning bolt shoot down my spine. Goosebumps flood my skin. *How could this be?* "Annie! You rascal! You have heard every single thing I have said, haven't you!?" I don't know comatose, but maybe the doctors don't know as much as they think they do either.

I was summoned back to the hospital at about 2 a.m. by a phone call from Fr. Lavin. When I arrive, Fr Lavin stands on one side of the bed anointing her and praying over her. I move to the other side of the bed and hold her hand. "I love you, Annie. You are the best friend I have ever had. Ever COULD have"

A sacred feeling, so solemn, so silent, so strong washes over me as Annie takes her final breath.

FRED SOUCIE

Fred Soucie is a retired trial lawyer in Anoka Minnesota. Between them, Fred and his wife Linda have seven daughters which, Fred explains, is why he has no hair.

In the past Fred has been recognized as an attorney of the year in Minnesota though he always introduces himself as a "humble servant of justice". He means it. He has taught lawyers "it's got to be about your client NOT about you."

Fred loves to spend time with Linda anywhere on earth,especially at their cabin getaway in Northern Minnesota.

Fred is a passionate football fan of UST in St. Paul where he played and where he received such strong support and love he credits for his success as a lawyer and a family man.

4

WHAT ARE YOU WAITING FOR?

CHRISTY JAYNES

*I*n one spontaneous moment, I packed up and moved to Richmond, Virginia to attend the art school at VCU. I had not yet been accepted, but that didn't stop me from renting an apartment on Franklin close to the university. Waiting for permission has not always been my strong suit. I knew what I wanted and was sure that admissions would want this for me, too. Art was my thing and clearly, they would recognize that.

Richmond turned out to be a string of interesting, if not crazy, capers, and one not-so-crazy boyfriend who was my anchor. Several months in, and before I had really begun to make Richmond my place, I found myself ditching VCU to move to Austin, Texas, with my parents. The invitation to move with my family came at a moment when I needed a little intervention. I had been a passenger in a car accident and was struggling quietly with chronic pain, which made working difficult, thinking hard, and creating impossible. I needed relief, and this was it.

"Out of all fifty states, why Texas? Have you heard how they talk down there?" I said to my dad, with an air of ignorance and youthful disgust.

"Austin is different. You'll like it," was his reply, and by and large, he was right.

It was 1993, and I was twenty-one, living at home again. My parents had purchased a five-acre ranchette just outside Austin, which was lovely, but not the place to be for a gal like me. I needed to be in the city where all of the *Slacker* action was happening.

First, I needed to get a job. In those days, that meant looking in the newspaper. For me, that was the Austin Chronicle, a local weekly paper filled with forward-thinking editorials, listings of all things arts and music, my horoscope, and the want ads. If you wanted a cool job, you had to look in a cool place. Just a bit of poking around yielded cool job option number one:

Photographer's Assistant
Experienced, able to carry
heavy equipment. flexible schedule
FT $30k salary, +health insurance

This ticked many cool boxes. I called, and the photographer answered and invited me for an interview the next day. So far, so good.

I dressed in my best 90s interview outfit, platform slides, and an acrylic shirt dress from Urban Outfitters and drove to Austin's east side. At the time, East Austin was a little less polished and a whole lot more fascinating. When I found the address (how did we even do that before GPS?), the building stuck out from the others along the street. It stood modern and tall in an area of town that was pretty neglected.

Unsure whether to knock or walk right in, I opened the door and looked in. The space was a live/work studio, open, airy, and full of expensive equipment. I could hear a voice, a man talking on the phone in another room, so I walked into the main space to see if I could catch his eye without calling out and interrupting his conversation. A tall, middle-aged man was pacing around on the phone, caught a glimpse of me, and waved for me to look around. The place was cool: a high-end studio that was clean, organized, and even sported a watercooler. Overall, it was a dreamy place; I could envision working there.

After hanging up the phone, he strode into the studio and asked if he could take me to lunch. We took separate cars. I followed him even further into the east side, to a tiny, dingy building with a low roof line and a thick coat of bright yellow paint. *Classy,* I thought sarcastically.

This is where I'd like to take a minute to point out that I grew up in the north, like all the way north, like kissing Canada north, and I didn't know shit when it came to what's good about Mexican culture or Mexican cuisine.

So we sat in a torn up vinyl booth—torn up like a hole in the seat so big I had to clench to keep from sliding in. He spoke Spanish to the waitress, with whom he was clearly friends, and two bowls of soup appeared in front of us. I figured I wasn't ordering off the menu. But it was free, so who was I to complain?

He began to ask me questions. At first, they were simple and illegal interview questions, like how old was I? But maybe this wasn't an interview? Maybe we are just having lunch? At this point, I was more distracted by the large chicken foot half-submerged in the broth and I wondered if this was a joke or something.

I've been to some crazy job interviews, like the one for a magician's assistant, where the interview was in a dark, empty auditorium. When I arrived, no one was there. I stood on the stage because that was the only lit space in the room. Surrounded by props and trunks, I waited for the magician to arrive. After showing up a bit late, he announced that the interview was two parts, handed me a heavy, crystal-bead-encrusted bodysuit, and told me to go put it on. The costumes had to fit me if I was to get the job.

Er, ok.

I stepped behind a black velvet curtain in a dark corner, took off my clothes, and stepped into the bodysuit; it fit. I came out, and the magician looked at me with a discerning eye and told me to turn, and I did.

"It fits," he muttered. "Now, let's see if you can do the two hardest tricks."

What?!

"Okay," I said, stepping forward.

He led me to a guillotine. (You read that right; the old timey kind used to chop people in half.) He explained how the entire act would work, what he would say to the audience, what my role was, and how the timing worked. Then he locked the guillotine around my middle, counted down, and on cue, I let out a Hollywood style, Academy-award-winning scream that should have had people running in from miles around to save me. No one did. After that, I levitated perfectly, and I got the job.

So this interview with the floating chicken foot, though it was odd, wasn't totally freaking me out. We squeezed wedges of lime into our soup and moved into regular conversation. I asked him questions about his business, and we began to chat more easily. I could actually see myself enjoying working for this guy because although he was a bit intimidating, what with his tall, handsome, easy-going confidence oozing everywhere, he was also kind and funny.

He continued with the interview questions. "What do you really want to do with your life? Like really?"

"Really, really? Travel," I confessed a bit shyly.

"Why don't you?"

"Money," I said between slurps as I navigated around the chicken foot.

"Well, then, get some money," he said so casually it hurt.

"That's why I'm here talking to you." I caught his gaze and smiled.

"Do you own that car out there?" He gestured at my white 1985 Buick Century.

"Yes."

"Sell it. Go somewhere. Stop waiting for life to happen to you. Don't do it right, just do it."

Now, I implore you to replay those words again with a Javier Bardem accent. Only then will you get the gravity, the full impact, the complete world-view-altering blow they made on me that day as he sat casually draped across that crappy vinyl booth.

Sell it.

Go somewhere

Stop waiting for life to happen to you.

Don't do it right, just do it.

"You can have this job if you want it. I think you should travel."

I went home to think about it. What I thought was: a thirty thousand dollar salary for a twenty-one-year-old gal in 1993 sounded enticing. But there are a few things I also knew: He liked me, he wanted to sleep with me and I would sleep with him, it would get messy, and the money and the health insurance and the coolness of the job didn't really mean anything because it was all just a big fucking game, in a light-filled studio, on the east side of Austin. So I called him, thanked him for the opportunity, and the good advice, and told him I was going to travel.

It's funny how easily we adopt suggestions that speak to our true nature. I took that man's words to heart. I did sell my car, I did move across the country, found work at a mountain resort, and I did stop waiting for life to happen to me. I was young and wanted to live a bold life, and for the most part, I did. But there was still a part of me that needed permission to go for it, to follow my passions, to cut out some of the more laborious steps society would prescribe for me to get from point A to point B.

Adopting philosophies like, "stop waiting for life to happen to you" sounds way easier than it actually is, even if you want to live that way and prefer the results. Sometimes, we take wild side roads on our way to our ultimate goal. Sometimes, the side roads don't seem to connect but are actually stepping stones, little lessons we'd eventually need to be able to make our ultimate leap to achieve a dream.

Throughout my work life, I've taken lots of wild side roads and tried new things out of curiosity or necessity, and while many of those things seem unrelated to my ultimate life goals, they somehow tie in perfectly. When it comes to jobs, the map goes something like this: babysitter, cobbler (a person who repairs shoes), summer theater spotlight operator and props finder, dancewear salesperson (think fitting ballerinas with toe shoes), light and sound designer for live productions, stage manager for plays and dance productions, drink girl at the Salt Lick Barbeque restaurant in Driftwood, Texas, vacuum cleaner salesperson (one vacuum sold), newspaper telemarketer selling local newspaper subscriptions, dishwasher at the officer training school at Quantico in Virginia, salesperson at Sam Goodie (you might remember the stores at the mall that sold records, tapes, and CDs), innkeeper in Bozeman, Montana, front desk person at a resort in Big Sky, front desk person at the haunted Driskill Hotel, front desk person at an Aveda salon, and head of HR for an infomercial product fulfillment center. I danced at a strip club for exactly one night (my Pink Pony Club moment), sold futons, held a whole list of buying and merchandising positions, was an assistant to some VPs at an advertising agency that handled some very compelling accounts, and then I became a mother and parenting coach.

There were only a few more jobs between that and becoming self-employed.

When I was around four years old, I'd set up my bedroom like a shop, lining up my toys on my bed and the bookshelf my dad had built and my mother had painted to create a display of "merchandise." My parents then dutifully shopped at my store with a stack of pennies and purchased items that "really caught their eye." This game was created from my fascination with shopkeepers and the wondrous worlds they would create. In those years, we lived on Whidbey Island in the Puget Sound. Small towns with small shops dot the perimeter of the fifty-mile-long island. One shop in particular, the Star Store, a multi-level, many-themed emporium in Langley, Washington, captivated my imagination and set in motion a lifelong desire to have a store of my own.

In my twenties, I journaled about the style and contents of my dream store, filling the pages with ideas and visualizations of teapots and stacks of books, blankets, and candles occupying my shelves. Around this time, I came across the book, *Creative Visualization*, by Shakti Gawain. I learned how to create a world in my mind, something I had always naturally done but now could accomplish with more purpose and intention. Creative visualization is at the core of everything that comes into my life.

When I was twenty-three, I told a co-worker what I thought the company's owners should do with all of their stores to improve sales.

He rolled his eyes and said, "You'll never tell them."

Dead-faced, I walked over to the phone, called headquarters, and asked the receptionist to transfer me to the owner, who I asked to lunch the next day. Fast forward a week, I had an office at headquarters, a company Amex card, and a plane ticket to New York City for a buying trip because I was now a furniture and accessories buyer for eight stores. Had I ever been a buyer? Nope. Had I ever been to New York? No. Did it all work out? Yep, quite well. That was the best retail education I could have received.

The decision to be self-employed, convince others to invest their money in your dreams, and commit to doing everything possible to make it a success is a ginormous leap. This kind of leap takes a deep well of resilience born of mindfulness, willingness, a dose of self-awareness, deep gratitude, and a supportive community. One day, it all just came together inside of me and outside of me, and more than thirty years after I'd set-up my bedroom shop and sold toys to my parents, I opened a big girl store.

At the time, I was married to a man who was as stoked about the idea as I was. I didn't realize just how committed he was to the idea until one day he picked me up from school (I'd gone back to college to get a degree in Anthropology) and asked if he could take me to look at something. He drove to a part of town I'd never been to and showed me an old building that was being renovated to house retail spaces.

"I know this sounds crazy right now, but what do you think of opening a store in this space?" he asked.

At first, I didn't know how to respond. I wondered how serious he was but noticed that I'd never seen him like this. He was serious and excited, maybe a little scared too. And right there, right then, I said yes to our future store.

When we say "yes" to something in life, the universe conspires to give us exactly what we need. Out of nowhere, we secured the loan we needed to open the shop from none other than his mom. It would never have occurred to me in a million years that his mother would want to invest in a business, and yet, a few days later, she wrote us a check for a hundred thousand dollars. Game on.

Don't do it right. Just do it.

We signed the lease, picked a name, found a designer to assemble our brand and logo ideas, and procured the goods to fill our shop. We worked hard assembling displays, setting up the computer system, unboxing, pricing, and merchandising all of our new treasures. The shop was in an old brick warehouse-style building with tall ceilings and lazy fans, which now housed a curated collection of modern furniture, art, candles, textiles, books, housewares, gifts for children, gifts for everyone, letter-pressed cards, jewelry, and more. I explored themes like raising chickens, beekeeping, urban gardening, bike culture, mid-century designers, and all things handmade and well-designed. We pulled it all together in just three short months, and then, one sunny September day, we officially opened.

I've never had more fun working in my life than when I worked in that shop. We started off strong with a community event that brought thousands of new faces through the door, word spread, and we had a nice little foothold in the community by the time December rolled around. But the morning that Larry Himmel, a beloved local news personality, rolled up to the shop with his cameraman and asked if he could shoot a piece about holiday shopping was the day everything exploded in the best way possible.

Larry Himmel changed my life forever with a simple interview that morning. When the news came several years later that he had passed, I sobbed and sobbed. He was an absolute angel in my life, instrumental in making my biggest dream come true.

Owning a shop is not an easy job and an even worse business plan. The idea is that you rent a room, buy a ton of stuff to fill that room, and then sit behind a counter and wait for people to find you and find something they like so much they need to buy it. What are the chances? It's bananas to think that we could create our dream, and then everyone would show up to help make that dream real, but that's how all of this works, all the time, every day, whether we're aware of it or not. And the Larry Himmels, local shoppers, and product designers and makers were all a part of my dream while dreaming their own dreams. All we have to do is say yes and take the first step.

The shop was everything I visualized and more. For a short time after, I had a sort of effervescent experience that every day, I was exactly where I needed to be, like my potential was being met, and my purpose had made its way to the surface and was being realized. Each morning, I felt like I was walking on air as I crossed the street, from the cafe where I picked up my morning coffee and croissant to my store. Our shop did very well. Our shop was quite popular. Our shop was at the center of a retail movement.

And then it all ended—for me at least.

Terrified I was about to break something I could not repair, I told my eleven-year-old daughter I was leaving her dad. I had rehearsed this conversation, never really comfortable with my narrative. She looked at me, and she listened, and she replied, "sometimes you just have to make a bold move, Mom." This is Maggie Jaynes in a nutshell. She's unexpected, wise, and insightful, and is the one person I will credit with spurring my constant personal evolution.

Divorce would cause me to give away my half of the shop just to get away from my husband. I truly believed that if I did it once, I could do it again, and so without negotiation, I legally gave him my share and left. When we "stop waiting for life to happen to us," it isn't always as glamorous as selling the car to travel; sometimes, it looks like deciding to leave a situation to create a new life.

Leaving my marriage and giving up my dream shop was the hardest decision I have ever made. It felt kind of like a death—of me, of us, of my little shop dreams. At the same time, I was filled with a new hope that the dream I had to be free from the dark side of our relationship and to walk through life being true to who I was, was about to become a reality.

In my new freedom, I began to consult and coach regularly; I also continued to pick up interior design jobs for businesses and homes. I worked with a huge variety of clients and loved my new direction.

Maybe as a salve to my soul, I turned back to my favorite kind of work and eventually opened another little shop, Kiko and Sven. A tiny and sweet boutique stuffed with clothing and jewelry, books, journals, candles, chocolate, lotions and perfumes, and gifts for all kinds of occasions. Oh, and plants, lots of plants. This time I did it without a large investor loan. This was more of a wing-and-aprayer type of venture, but it worked. The shoppers showed up, the media showed up, and once again something that started as a fantasy, a grand idea, became a reality because so many people said yes to me.

Eventually, I sold my tiny shop to become a caregiver, student, coach, and artist, not in equal parts. These days, self-employment looks different. I have a micro design agency and coach women in business and career building. I paint and occasionally sell my art and help my now-husband, Joseph, with his therapy practice. All of these things add up to another dream I hold: the dream of autonomy and closeness with Joseph and our little dogs. I can work at my desk, then step outside into our garden for a break. I only choose clients I love to work with on projects I believe in. It's not flashy, but it's perfect for me.

I often thought about that afternoon in the little yellow cafe with chicken foot soup, especially when I found myself feeling unhappy in a way that I can't quite understand. It made me ask the questions, "What should I be doing, trying, seeking that I am not? What am I putting off, or pushing down, or saving for later?" The truth was I don't always know what I want, what I'm seeking or saving for later, and that lack of clarity stopped me short when it was time to take action. I think that was what the photographer meant by "waiting for life to happen *to* you."

When I recognize that I've fallen into the sleepless dream of waiting for life, snapping out of it has become so much easier. Waiting for life to change or deliver a dream has a quality that feels like deprivation, it's easy to spot.

Waiting is a simple concept to understand, which equates to expecting something while doing nothing, but I've learned that there are different kinds of waiting in this life. There's the waiting I've done for things that never come: apologies, understanding, recognition, justice, love from someone I so badly wished would love me, even a little. Then there are the things I waited too long for, like getting divorced, seeking help for the trauma caused by a violent event, and waiting on a handful of dreams for reasons I cannot remember.

The opposite of waiting is taking action, which requires many more faculties, ones I had to cultivate over time. The moments when my clarity and willingness converged to move me toward something new and even a little scary mark the map of my life like cairns on a hillside. Perfectly balanced to endure the seasons, a cairn is a stack of stones that marks the way for travelers. When I stack together clarity, willingness, resilience, and optimism, I get a sign pointing the way forward, a shortcut that leads me ever closer to the life I want.

CHRISTY JAYNES

Christy Jaynes is a renowned coach specializing in helping women navigate career transitions, offering expert guidance on decision-making, personal branding, and turning talents into marketable products. With a proven track record of empowering women to leverage their expertise, Christy's coaching has transformed countless careers. As a bestselling author, she is currently working on her full-length book, further establishing her as a thought leader in her field.

In her free time, Christy indulges her passion for painting, creating and selling her art. Her multifaceted career and creative endeavors inspire many to pursue their professional and personal dreams with confidence and clarity.

https://www.linkedin.com/in/christy-jaynes-a3740814/
https://www.christyjaynes.com/

5

TO LOVE THE UNLOVED

NATASHA CAMPISI

*T*he day everything changed started just like any other. My mom pulled into the garage, the familiar rumble of our minivan marking the end of another school day for my brother and me. Outside, our neighborhood remained the same grim spectacle it had always been—streets marred by graffiti, rival gangs waging their relentless turf wars, and the ever-present hum of tension that clung to the air like an unwelcome shadow. I hated living in the hood.

Once, our neighborhood had seemed like an average middle-class community, but over time, it transformed into something straight out of an Eazy-E and Ice Cube lyric. Our family had managed to carve out a semblance of comfort amidst the chaos, but it felt increasingly surreal. Despite my father's success as a graphic artist, the designer clothes we wore, the family camping trips, and our little piece of paradise with the community pool, I couldn't shake the sense of disconnection. We were like a picture-perfect postcard wedged into the middle of a war zone, an illusion of normalcy in a world that felt anything but. A voice inside always questioned why we still lived in this run-down city.

On the outside, our home was a grand illusion—a perfect exterior hiding a reality my parents worked tirelessly to mask. The world saw a family in sync, while within our walls, it was a struggle to find harmony. The relative luxury of our house was real, but the warmth of our home, as it turned out, was something we had yet to find. Our life seemed enviable to friends—like a scene plucked from a Home and Garden magazine. To me, home life felt like it desperately needed an intervention on the Dr. Phil show.

The contradictions within our household were stark. My father, my world's center, was a source of profound love and confusing behavior. His fixation on control—from spying on our phone calls to dictating my mother's every move—created an atmosphere of fear and disappointment. His stubborn refusal to move us to a safer area, despite our pleas, was a familiar torment. We were trapped in a cycle of discontent, where questioning our circumstances felt like a waste of time.

One afternoon, as I arrived home from school, a friend approached me with a seemingly innocent invitation—to meet a guy she had a crush on, who wanted to show off his new motorcycle. Her excitement was palpable, but something in my gut was screaming a warning, a piercing alarm that shocked me with intensity. But I wasn't aware enough to trust this voice, so I ignored it, convinced that supporting my friend was the right thing to do, especially in the tight-knit, dangerous world where having each other's backs was the unspoken rule.

We arrived at a house in an unfamiliar part of town. My friend's crush greeted us with a casual grin, but standing beside him was another figure—a known gang member whose reputation for violence preceded him. His appearance was grotesque, a disconcerting mask of decay and menace. His sunken eyes and acne-scarred face told a story of darkness and aggression that set my nerves on edge. Ill-fitting pants hung off him like ragged drapes. My body began to feel sick; my mind kept ignoring my gut as it told me to leave.

Despite my growing unease, I stayed, waiting for my friend as she took a ride on the motorcycle. The minutes stretched into what felt like hours, and with each passing second, my anxiety mounted. Panic began to seep in, a gnawing sense that something was terribly wrong.

Fear began to yell, "She's not coming back." What do I do? I scanned my options to escape as my mind desperately struggled not to drown in fear.

Suddenly, I heard a raspy voice behind me.

"Let's wait in the garage for them. They'll be back soon."

"No, I'd rather wait outside, thank you."

My body clenched instantly, as if it were trying to protect me from the inevitable. His requests shifted into commands, and my gut screamed at me to run, but the thought of fleeing felt more terrifying than staying put. In the world I knew, blending in with the hood was a survival tactic, even though every fiber of my being despised it. I learned to fake comfort with the life around me, to play a part I hated.

The stench of sweat emanating from him made me want to bolt, but my mind quickly overruled my instincts. *Maybe he means well*, it reasoned, trying to soften the reality of his terrorizing presence. *Beneath that scarred face, perhaps he's not so bad*. My thoughts had become a dictator, much like my father's overbearing control at home. I submitted to the gang member's demands with the same resignation my mother had when navigating my father's volatile moods, hoping to avoid confrontation.

Numbly, I agreed and followed him to the garage. Each step felt like a betrayal of my safety.

He pushed the door open with a creak that seemed to echo in my head. As I cast a swift glance inside, he shoved me roughly into the darkness, slamming the door shut with a loud bang. The clatter of the deadbolt sliding into place was a final, ominous click.

Panic surged through me as I reached out, trying to push him aside to escape, but his hand shot out, closing around my neck with a vice-like grip.

"If I open this door," he whispered in my ear, his voice cold and threatening, "my guard dog will be set loose." His words were a chilling promise, and a wave of terror swept over me. I felt frigid and suffocated.

Conflicting, jarring thoughts erupted in my mind, a screeching alarm that clawed at my thoughts, drowning out the trust I forced myself to have.

I opened my mouth to scream, but his hand slammed over it with brutal force, the pressure cutting off my breath.

A chilling dread twisted in my stomach, a primal warning that something horrific was imminent. If I had any chance of survival, surrender seemed my only option.

As I turned my gaze into the garage, the scene that greeted me was one of disgust: a filthy couch surrounded by discarded trash and crumpled boxes, enveloped in darkness. The air was filled with the stench of rotting food, a sickening reminder of neglect and decay, the exact stench this man's aura reeked of. Standing in the darkness, numbness crept through my body, as though shock was weaving its way into my bones.

He shoved me onto the couch with a force that sent me flat onto my back. My right hand instinctively reached for the couch's torn upholstery, seeking any comfort it might offer against the crushing weight of his body pressing down on me. His physical strength, bolstered by his terrifying reputation for cruelty, overpowered every ounce of resistance in me. I felt a cold, penetrating numbness creep through my limbs, my body trembling and helpless. I was utterly at his mercy, paralyzed with fear and uncertainty about what he would do next.

Inside, my thoughts became foggy, a blur. A ghostly slideshow of my life began parading before me—fragmented memories of joy flashing in desperate haste, as though something within was trying to gift me slivers of happiness before my final breath in this cold, unforgiving garage.

I felt a burn down the left side of my hip, and I quickly realized he found the zipper on the side of my pants, and it had caught on my skin. He forced it down my hip, and I felt the skin ripping as the zipper was forced open.

He pulled my pants off and covered my mouth with his hand. He entered me, and I felt my soul separate from the physical me as I blacked out. Suddenly, I was floating in the air. I could sense I was still alive, but my body, my home, was being violated. My inner voice whispered, "It's not safe; wait here."

When surrendering control to stay alive, minutes feel like hours. It felt as if my mind fainted while my body remained alive. This was the start of a dissociative reality that would become my life after this death.

Every facet of my being felt brutally dishonored. The already fragile notions of love and personal boundaries were incinerated, leaving only smoldering remnants of shame in my mind. This stranger extinguished every glimmer of hope I once cherished.

His labored, demonic breath washed over my face as he finished. I dragged my fractured consciousness back to the present. *I'm here, alive but numb. I must remain motionless, pretend to accept the atrocity that has befallen me.* The only thought consuming me was the desperate need to escape.

He got off me. I pulled my pants up quickly and got up from the couch. I couldn't zip my pants because the zipper was broken. I had to hold my pants up. He walked over to the door and opened it. I ran out and never looked back.

I felt heavy, like I was dragging a dead body with me. My mind had no idea how to get home, but my body led the way. As I panic-walked, I began to feel wet warm semen dripping down my right leg like poison seeping out of my body. The venom of this monster was inside of me and there was nothing I could do to get it out. I began to walk faster, hoping the slow jog would make it come out faster.

I made it to the front door of my house. I saw my mom in the kitchen and my little brother watching TV in the living room. *Life inside this home is so different from life outside these walls, I think to myself. We don't belong here. We are so different from the people outside. Or maybe we are alike. Maybe that's why my father feels at home here.*

As I tried to make sense of the terror that had happened, the paradox of life began to artfully craft multiple realities in my mind which somehow soothed the adrenaline still pumping through my body.

Weeks slipped by, and the night's horrors seemed to fade, or so I convinced myself. With eighth-grade graduation approaching, the boy I'd been crushing on finally asked me to the dance. Elation filled me, and for a moment, life felt like it might return to its pre-trauma rhythm. Being asked to the dance felt almost dreamlike. Perhaps I could bury the past and move on.

Everything seemed on track until I missed my period. Panic gripped me again—there was no way I was late. I must have miscalculated. I was a virgin before this. How could I be pregnant that fast? This must be a mistake. Babies are born from love. This wasn't how I imagined becoming a mother. My mind went wild with horrific "what if's".

My childhood best friend was the only person I could confide in. Her shock mirrored mine. We rushed to the local pharmacy for a pregnancy test. Back at her house, I darted into the bathroom with the kit, my body trembling uncontrollably. I barely managed to pee on the stick. All I wanted was to vanish, escape this body that felt tainted. My mind scrambled for an escape route but there wasn't one.

Yup, my worst nightmare was happening. I was pregnant. My mind began to shame me. *God does not love me. Why else would he allow this to happen to me? I am carrying a child conceived by evil. I created life from being raped. What is wrong with me?*

My mind came to the conclusion that I was unloved. If I were loved, I'd be loved. What happened to me was not love.

Going forward with this pregnancy would be a lifetime reminder of that night—an imminent path to suicide. If God didn't love me, I would do my best to pick up his slack. I chose to abort the pregnancy secretly.

After the abortion, I felt utterly disembodied. The world felt like it had slipped into a blurry haze, a smudged watercolor painting where the edges of everything blurred into one another. After the trauma, I felt as though I was no longer fully anchored to my own existence. I became a spectator in my own story, disconnected from the emotions and experiences that once made me feel alive.

It was as if my identity had been fractured, leaving me to navigate a world where I was both present and absent, engaged yet detached. The rape had pulled me from the center of my life and left me orbiting on the periphery, struggling to reconnect with a self that felt increasingly foreign and out of reach.

I wanted to appear normal. I wanted to forget. I wanted to move on.

A few months after the rape, I met a guy who I quickly fell in love with. From the moment we met, it was like

God conspired to make me feel special again. He made me feel wanted, his attention intense and flattering. His attention melted away any reservations I might have had.

It was exhilarating the way he pursued me with relentless excitement, it made me feel special. I was swept up in the whirlwind of happy emotions I wasn't used to. It was intoxicating and enchanting, a life that seemed too good to be true. Best of all, I wasn't alone anymore. I was finally wanted. I was infatuated with his charisma; how he made me feel was nothing short of addictive.

But beneath the surface of this enchanting exterior lay a dark reality. The charm that once felt like a blessing slowly revealed itself to be a tool of manipulation and control. He had a way of making me feel like everything was my fault, twisting my words and actions until I was left questioning my sanity. Arguments that initially seemed like normal disagreements, became battlegrounds where he would belittle me, making me feel small and insignificant. His words cut deep, and the emotional wounds were slow to heal, masked by his periodic attempts to make amends with grand gestures that felt more like an obligation than genuine remorse.

What started as an illusionary first love turned into a shotgun marriage my father forced because I was pregnant and underage. I ended up in a sixteen-year, severely abusive marriage that almost cost me my life after a gun misfired during one of his violent attempts to kill me.

Shame spent decades relentlessly manifesting unforgiving scenes of dishonoring and devaluing myself. Unaware, I perpetually rejected and betrayed the parts of me that yearned to be loved by seeking validation through the lens of lack and abuse.

In the dimly lit corners of my life, a destructive belief system lurked like a shadow, silently weaving its way into my life. I was an emotionally homeless woman starving for love, digging in trash dumpsters searching for rotten leftovers, which became my definition of love.

Abuse became a twisted form of intimacy, where the bar for what I thought I deserved was set impossibly low. I convinced myself that any form of attention, even harmful, was better than the emptiness I felt within.

At the age of thirty-three, in the aftermath of the divorce, my relationships with men felt like a series of echoing heartbreaks, each one eerily familiar and unsettlingly similar. I wandered through the dating landscape with a disoriented sense of déjà vu, drawn repeatedly to the same patterns of hurt and betrayal, as if I were trapped in a loop I couldn't escape.

Trauma had left me with a fractured sense of self-worth, and I clung to the notion that if I just tried harder, if I were more accommodating, things might change. I became a chameleon, altering myself to fit the mold of what I thought each man wanted, hoping that love would somehow reward my efforts. Faking it for love became a far more self-deceptive mantra than faking it to stay safe in the hood.

The voice always started softly, like a distant whisper barely audible over the dissonance of my thoughts.

"This isn't right," it said, not with judgment but with a quiet firmness that felt like a gentle hand guiding me through a fog. The voice was mine but somehow separate, a clear-eyed observer amidst the chaos of fear and emotions. It was not shouting but rather speaking with a calm conviction that resonated deeply within me.

In countless moments, I'd been accustomed to silencing this inner voice, pushing it away as I made excuses or hoped life would magically improve effortlessly. But now, this voice felt like an anchor in the storm, grounding me in a truth I had long been reluctant to face.

"You deserve more than this," it continued, with each word a soothing balm to my battered soul.

The same voice that wondered why we still lived in the hood questioned why I allowed myself to be unloved by others. A voice that wouldn't give up whenever I was on the floor picking up the pieces of a broken heart. What seemed like a noise in my mind was really the voice of my heart arousing thought-provoking questions in hopes of being seen, heard, and loved by me.

This is the same voice that pierced through many moments of hopelessness, "Believe you can be for your children the mother you wish you had, the role model you wish you had, the love you wish you had and the light you wish you felt. Be the provider you want to have. Be the safety you didn't have. Be the voice you wish you had." This was the breath that kept me from giving up on life. This flame was my inner beloved loving me.

Creating a relationship with this inner beloved was like nurturing a delicate seedling. I approached it with both reverence and curiosity, learning to recognize its gentle guidance amidst the clamor of old insecurities and fears. The voice was a source of wisdom and compassion I had often sought in external validation but was now finding within.

As I began to act on the inner voice's guidance, the results were not always immediate or apparent. There were moments of failure, of setbacks that made me question whether I had made a mistake. Yet, each time I returned to the quiet space of introspection, the voice remained unwavering, offering comfort and clarity. Through these experiences, I started to see the value in trusting this inner guidance. The more I listened, the more I recognized patterns and insights that proved to be surprisingly accurate.

Building trust with this inner voice required patience and a willingness to let go of old habits. I had to learn to differentiate between the voice of genuine intuition and the louder, more critical voices that had dominated my thoughts for so long. This involved a deepening self-awareness and a commitment to self-compassion. The inner voice spoke with a gentleness that contrasted sharply with the harsh judgments I had been accustomed to telling myself.

The process in learning to trust myself was not linear; as there were times when doubts resurface, and I questioned the voice's wisdom. However, I found a profoundly affirming sense of peace and alignment each time I trusted it and followed its guidance. I was learning to see this inner voice not as an intrusive whisper but as a wise, nurturing presence that was with me, always waiting to be acknowledged.

Over time, this inner voice was becoming a steadfast companion, guiding me through the complexities of life with a clarity and confidence I had never known before. It taught me true wisdom often comes from within and learning to trust oneself is an ongoing journey of self-discovery and inner alignment. Over the years, this voice taught me how to be an incredible mother to my three kids. She kept my heart soft throughout the harshness of life. I learned to believe in my higher purpose and my gifts. She challenges my comfort zones with an ambitious spirit that is eager to grow. She shows me glory in disrupting ancestral karma that plagued my life. She made me a healer. This voice built an unwavering relentlessness that overcame all the odds against me for as long as I can remember.

One of the most healing acts of self-love she taught me was the power of embracing forgiveness for my past mistakes. I had carried a heavy burden of guilt and regret for not listening to her thirty-three years ago when she yelled, "Don't go." I spent decades believing that I had to pay for every misstep with unrelenting self-criticism. But the inner voice taught me that forgiveness was not a weakness but a crucial step toward healing. I began to gently release the tremendous weight of my past, especially the rape, allowing myself to move forward with a sense of renewal and hope.

This journey was not a path to erasing the rape and abortion but to transforming it into a narrative of self-love. The trauma that once felt like an insurmountable obstacle became a trial through which I forged a deeper connection with myself. Each challenge and triumph deepened my understanding of who I am and what I deserve.

Looking back, I saw the journey the rapist set me on as a testament to the strength of my sovereignty and self-love. The inner voice that guided me through this transformation was a source of comfort and a powerful force that illuminated the path from darkness to light. In embracing my journey, I discovered that the true victory lay not in the absence of pain but in the ability to transform it into a source of profound personal growth and self-acceptance.

NATASHA CAMPISI

Natasha Campisi is a human empowerment healer, life coach and author. Her work weaves around transforming life through the power of storytelling. Her personal healing journey began in 2007 with a NDE that alchemized her path into becoming a healer. Since then, she has been immersed in multidisciplinary spiritual and energetic modalities such as shamanism, reiki, ancient art of Egyptian Ankhing, radiant heart meditation, energy healing, sound healing, breath work and womb healing.

During her journey in becoming a healer, Natasha works in finance and real estate sales. Her passion to serve still includes making homeownership dreams come true for her clients.

She is working on her most personal project to date, a novel about Iris, a hero born villain that embarks on a hero's journey traveling between timelines retelling her story to free herself and her lineages of the karmic cycles she helped create.

https://www.natashacampisi.com/
https://www.linkedin.com/in/natashacampisi/

6

THE REWRITE

SHAY MICHELLE DRAPEAU

*P*OP! POP! POP!

The sound of tires screeching signals the all-clear. My mother bursts into the bedroom we share to find me with my stomach still pressed to the carpet in front of the window.

"It's okay, Mel," she says calmly. "You can get up."

The curling iron she'd only used on a portion of her golden curls is still clutched in her hand. The cord dangles as she motions for me to follow her into the hall. My grandmother's soft eyes find me as she exits her room to join us. As two generations engulf me, I wonder to myself if the shooter—or perhaps the victim—is family, friend, or foe. The probability lost on my young mind.

Six drive-by shootings in less than a month. The frequency seems to be increasing.

I take a peek through our bedroom window, beyond the pinned-tight curtains to the almost desiccated land behind our house. Our backyard, once a sprawling haven for hide-and-seek games, barbecues, and birthdays, is a foreign land to me now. I ventured there a handful of times this summer, only to be shooed away by an elder.

"It's too dangerous," they'd said.

The garage is the only thing keeping bangers from running from the block beyond our backyard, through our green and dirt, down our driveway, to the safety of Pamplin Place. Who knows how long that mangled structure will keep them at bay?

"Is Danny out there?" I ask my mother. She now stands in the bathroom mirror, coiling a strand of hair around the piping-hot rod.

She pauses to turn awkwardly toward me with the curling wand held at her temple. "I don't know, baby."

"Do you think he would kill anybody?"

She turns back to the mirror, her eyes closed. "I hope not."

"Do you think someone will kill him?"

She breathes a deep sigh and mutters, "God give me strength," to herself before answering, "Why don't you go play with your cousin?"

The passage I had written was an excerpt from something I'd presented in my writing group. I'd chosen to write a fictional book about a boy and a girl who were best friends. It wasn't until I was a few chapters in, listening to others read and critique my pages, that I realized how closely the characters mimicked my life.

The boy and girl were based on me and my high school best friend. The book's main character lived in gangland St. Louis, while the fictional boy, like my best friend, lived in the suburbs. Like me, the female character had an older sibling figure involved in gangs and drugs but had turned his life around to become a positive part of the community. Also, like me, she had a younger sibling figure revered as more beautiful whom she protected. Unlike me, she had a two-parent household, something I'd always craved.

I wrote multiple passages that did not look like my life to separate myself from the nerdy young girl on the page. But I could not write the pages that mimicked my life. I knew those moments belonged. They were as important to the story as they were in my life. It became increasingly difficult to sit down in front of the computer and write. Every time I came to the keys, my legs tingled.

My chest burned. My heart echoed throughout my body. My hands vibrated as I reached for the keyboard.

The first time I witnessed a drive-by still sits vividly in my mind. I was helping my aunt bring groceries into the house. I hadn't even made it to her car to collect the first bag when I heard the tires screech as the gun fired off its shots. Gravel dug into my hands as I dropped after the first shot rang out. I watched from in between the concrete curb and my aunt's car as the white town car sped away. Screams from behind our house told me that the lingering crew beyond was the likely target.

The car raced down our street. Shots could be heard in the distance. I stayed in place until the ringing in my ears stopped and my aunt's sandaled feet rushed toward me.

The police came quickly, which was a shock to me. I'd never heard about the police coming after a drive-by. The two officers looked ten feet tall to my young eye. I stared straight ahead as they spoke to my aunt. The gun in the holster looked smaller than the gun I'd seen my cousin put high up on a shelf before he scolded me for being "a nosey little tattletale."

I heard from above the holster, "Did anybody see anything?"

The policeman had a squat nose and broad shoulders. He didn't look mean, just like he'd been punched in the face one too many times. I thought to myself, *I have as much power as the women who raised me. He doesn't look as scary as they do when you turn off their stories.* I raised my hand.

My aunt immediately grabbed my arm and shoved it back down. Confusion spun through my head.

"Naw. We ain't see nothing," I heard my aunt say.

Huh? Wasn't I supposed to tell the police what I saw? But then I remembered—snitches get stitches. Or did snitches end up in ditches?

I blocked out the rest of the exchange between my aunt and the police. She had moved me behind her, as the officer had surely noticed my projected arm. I watched the space up our driveway to the rickety garage, the only blockade to runners escaping through our property.

"Well, you let us know if you hear anything," the muscular man with blue eyes said.

"Yeah. Right," my aunt retorted.

When their squad car was more than a few houses down, she yanked me back by my arm.

"Don't you ever tell the police shit. You'll get your ass shot." Then she held me tight, taking me past my grandmother waiting on the porch.

At the time, I thought it was the police who would shoot me. It took a few more years and a few fallen friends before I learned there was something deadlier in my neighborhood.

No one died that day, but the guilt of not being allowed to tell what I saw still gnaws at my gut.

Latent post-traumatic stress syndrome. That's what my therapist called it, with a side of anxiety. I thought PTSD was only for soldiers who had seen war. Mine was from growing up in St Louis, Missouri, home of the Ferguson riots that were the result of the fatal shooting of Michael Brown by a Ferguson police officer. My cousin viewed Mike Brown's body from her window—laying under a covering for hours while her boys, similar in stature and perceived as an equal threat, played in their room. A room my son had slept in just one week before. That was where I was raised. That was where much of my family still lived. It was a place I still visited often despite the trauma I incurred there.

Why doesn't my family have PTSD? How can they have *post*-traumatic syndrome when they are *presently* living in my trauma?

The only people I knew with a college degree outside of teachers were Dorian, my dad's brother, and my mom's sister, Sharon. My uncle was a lawyer, and I revered his penchant for standing up to the man on behalf of the little guy. (And his massive house.) My aunt and namesake worked at Anheuser-Busch; I saw her as the most prominent member of my mother's family. She was both envied and chastised for being bougie or better than —for being educated and making something of herself. I coveted that.

St. Louis, Missouri, is a place I always knew I'd escape. My aunt Sharon helped me prepare for career advancement by teaching me how to conduct myself in a job interview, format my resume, and position myself among my peers at career and internship fairs. Uncle Dorian called me *Joe College* and prepped me for life beyond the Mississippi River every time we spoke.

"Here's a book on scholarships," he'd said, handing me a thick book at the local library.

I traced the words *College Prep*.

When my cousins began going off to college, I noted the difference between those who left and the ones who stayed. I knew leaving St. Louis was the only way to be seen as talented and educated *without* being shunned or judged for my accomplishments. I applied to several local colleges but knew I would end up in New York. My father was there. My uncle, who had his cool gigs as a musician, was there. His daughter was already in New York attending college.

"You Bells are so arrogant," my grandmother, GG, would say of my father's family.

I sat with her shelling walnuts one Thanksgiving. I hated walnuts, but I loved sitting with her. I watched her strong, brown hands as she took two hard casings and cracked them together. She pulled the flesh from the debris. My amateur hands weren't strong enough to crack two together for as long as she did. I always ended up using the nutcracker. GG ate a few walnuts occasionally, but most went into the large bowl between us for pies or to sit on the table.

"Why do you always say that, GG?" I was visiting from college. I'd been going on and on about a business law class I'd aced, proud of my accomplishment.

"You think 'cause you went off to that school, your cousins ain't got sense?"

I'd suggested some ideas to my cousin for his business, only to be dismissed. I guess the family grapevine made its way to our grandmother.

"I never said that, GG."

"But you think it."

Silence.

"Hmph. You got school sense. Plenty. Common sense, sometimes. But they got sense about things you don't. Just like you know things they don't."

I'd always felt like an odd duck in St. Louis. Different from the cousins I'd been raised with. A quiet yet argumentative nerd in a family of jocks, jokers, and survivors. We were family. We gossiped or caught up when we managed to call one another. Our emotions for each other ran deep. We had a shared history that bonded us forever, but I never understood how the ones who chose to stay could stand it. The moment my high school diploma hit my hand, I made a break for it.

Most thought that by choosing a school in New York, I'd be in the middle of the hustle and bustle. Times Square, Port Authority, subway rides, and the humans of New York were a bit too much for me. Too loud, busy, and unpredictable. I chose to attend a small women's college in Westchester, NY. It was close enough to New York City to enjoy the chaos, culture, and nightlife, but it was far enough away that my family couldn't drop in on me. I was finally in a place where no one knew me as the scared little nerd who sat alone in the corner. Sharon was gone. Shay was born.

Shay was loud, jovial, and made friends quickly. For the first time, she had trust and safety in Tarrytown, NY.

Bonding with my father during my college years in New York, I began working for his production company. I majored in theater and film to get my foot in the door of screenwriting and fell in love with the art of film editing. When I moved back to Westchester, NY, after starting a family, working for my father became more difficult. The commute to various locations was tedious with a work-from-home husband and a toddler.

I began volunteering at Larchmont-Mamaroneck Television (LMC-TV) a few times per week. It was a local access television station in Westchester, New York. I'd toured the studio and attended meetups as part of a film production Meetup group. After seeing two women, one about my age and the other a mom like me, run the inner workings, I worked up the courage to volunteer.

I'd been tasked with retrieving tapes from the main office housed in the village municipal building. Old VHS tapes containing B-roll and stock footage sat on racks.

"Oh! Are you the other Sharon? I heard about you!"

I'd introduced myself as Shay, but the woman, about six feet tall, stood and came around her desk. She smiled down her glasses at me.

"Nice to meet you," I said.

"I'm Sharon." Her New York accent was thick. The drawl of the New York "a" made *our* name sound like Shaahrin, but she was so pleasant I couldn't help the big smile on my face.

Her big personality matched her tall, welcoming stature. She reminded me of my aunts, but her cocoa skin was more akin to that of my grandmother. I was immediately drawn home.

Erik, our timid, white-haired boss, came out of his office. "The new Sharon? Hey Shay!"

I shook his outstretched hand. I'd met him before but wasn't about to mention that. Sharon raised an eyebrow, but I didn't question what that was about.

Excusing myself, I left with the tapes and a new work friend.

"You let me know if anybody bothers you," she told me on my way out.

I felt like she was the mama bear of LMC-TV, and I liked her instantly.

Sharon and I were the only two Black people I knew to work at LMC-TV—the only two Black women. Sharon hosted a TV show for the station and had been nominated for an award. But, like other women of LMC-TV, Sharon was chasing other creative pursuits.

It took me a few years and a pregnancy to tire of production life. Desiring the kind of recognition for my passion that Sharon received, I sought to return to the creative purpose I'd loved as a teen—writing. I knew I wanted to leave a legacy for my children. I'd been raised by powerful women and those who held me up through some of my most challenging times. I wanted to honor their stories, so the "She Breathes Life" blog was born.

The blog focused on the groups I was involved with and the women who frequented them. Interviews and guest blog posts supplemented my rantings and epithets on LGBTQI advocacy, parenting, and sisterhood. But blogging reignited a passion I'd forgotten in my race to motherhood. I'd found purpose in sharing women's accomplishments and survival stories. I wanted to be published and knew I needed encouragement and support.

Returning to Meetup to find writer's groups, I found one close enough to home to bring my kids when needed.

The writers sat at a grouping of tables arranged in a U shape. I chose a seat. As I made introductions with those nearest, I heard a familiar voice.

"Hi, everyone. Hi, Shay!" Sharon bounded into the room, her bag swinging as she jostled the chair out of her way to take up the space she needed. She beamed at me. I made my way over to her, accepting the warmth of her embrace.

"Haven't seen you in a while."

"Yeah," I grimaced. "I quit a few months ago."

I was pleased to see her there, and Sharon made me feel less nervous. I hadn't presented my writing to anyone in so long that I thought these people would judge me harshly. I felt like I'd failed in the realm of production and that many of the things I was doing at the time had nothing to do with my degree. I felt like I owed the universe an explanation, but seeing her there—seeing someone else from LMC-TV was also in a writing space —made me feel accepted. I began going to meetings regularly, and Sharon was encouraging.

One audacious day, I decided to write a full-length book, even though I'd yet to complete a short story. I thought a more significant challenge would get me over the hurdle. When I presented chapters to the group, I received good critiques. I was told that I was a good writer, that I was good at painting an image, and that I knew how to draw the scene with words.

Then, I felt reality bleeding into my fiction. A boulder weighed down my wrists as I sat, staring at the blinking cursor. My previous words taunted me from the screen.

I remember Sharon's words after confessing this experience, "The next time you sit down to write this story, I want you to pause. I want you to breathe, and I want you to *think* about why you can't write this story."

I did so. I sat at my desk. My pretty, mint, typewriter-style keyboard clacked beneath my fingers. The sound was a balm as my characters' dialogue about the mundane expanded.

"So how many is it?" Jackson looked like he'd discovered a secret room only teachers knew about, full of all the confiscated items we'd lost over the years.

I didn't know what to tell him; there was no thrill in living with guns in your house. He didn't live where I did. He didn't wish his neighbors were white with picket fences and yappy little dogs. He lived amongst manicured lawns and neighbors you weren't afraid to talk to. He didn't have to drive forty minutes to the 'good' mall. He didn't have to worry about slowing cars or stray bullets when mowing his lawn, and he probably hadn't been to three funerals in one year or had experienced gunshots at one.

The clacking slowed.

Staccato.

A few words here and there.

Dot, dot, dot....

My hands left the keys. Itchy. My heartbeat thrummed in my ears. My breath shortened. I couldn't stop the tears. I was washed with fear and shame. The fear was something from childhood, the shame of letting that fear consume me enough to halt my talents. How often had I been on the precipice of completion, only to abandon a work-in-progress due to panic? How many interested agents does it take before I bring my pitched manuscript to fruition?

I read the words on the page: gunshots at a funeral.

Had that happened? Had I been there?

I rubbed my hands on my jeans. Was it a buried memory, or was my imagination overdramatizing again? Reality bleeding into fiction? Or is fiction bleeding into reality? Even when your body communicates so clearly that there is a problem, it can still be hard to trust.

Panic set in.

Fear of violence. Fear of guns. Fear that at any moment, a bullet would fly through the window and pierce my flesh. I remembered the number of times I had to cower underneath the television or the window because all of a sudden—POP POP POP—and there I'd go, down on the floor, belly to the carpet next to the beautiful curtains that touched the floor.

I remember looking out on our backyard. The grass was so green. My mom used to pay someone to cut it, and I remember thinking, *Why? Nobody goes out there.* The last birthday party I remember having back there was my tenth. I barely had friends over once I was in high school because why would they come? When your house becomes a target for gang violence, your friend's mom doesn't want them at your home; that's understandable. I get that now that I'm a parent. I think I got it then. It may be why I insisted on going to them.

You could see through our backyard, through the fence, and through the parking lot on the other side to a house where gang members sat with large bottles of beer, saggy pants, and guns hanging out of their waistbands. Unless a car slowly drove by, they had no care in the world.

I cared.

I'd heard that a little girl had been shot through the wall of her bedroom while reading in her bed. She was about my age. Since I loved to read, I was terrified that it would be me, so I made a reading nook in my grandmother's pantry. My cousin and I would sit in there, in our world of snacks and holiday cutlery, while I read to her. I began venturing to the local library when we lost the nook due to a scary story mishap that terrified my cousin.

The library became my haven. I made that fifteen-minute walk any chance my mother would allow. I became obsessed with the written word. In the library, there were no thugs. I felt safe. Frequenting a library wasn't the thing to do if you were in a gang. The only guns were in books. The mightiest sword was the pen, and Black boys could live past sixteen. In the library, I learned to escape into the written word. I learned that you could rewrite your existence. Fallen friends filled blank pages as long as you had ink and the will to write.

My friendship with Sharon has bloomed over the years in the writer's group. She's gone from coworker to friend. Seeking nuggets whenever she spoke or poked fun, I allowed myself to be present and accept her as an adopted aunt.

Sharon doesn't know what she gave me on that day when she triggered the unlocking of held emotions and showed me that someone can change what it means to be a friend in just a few words.

Sharon's voice echoed in my ears months after my hands shook above my keyboard. It had been an earworm I couldn't dislodge. As my husband entertained the kids during my writing time, I meditated. A ringing in my ear, high pitched, canceled out all other noise. Then I saw it —precisely what I needed to do, thanks to Sharon.

We were at brunch—Sharon, Shavon, Stephanie, and me. It had become our monthly ritual to take turns choosing a location. I'd confessed that Sharon had inadvertently unlocked my PTSD.

"How can I write this knowing that it's me? My trauma?"

"It's your story, Shay," Sharon admonished. "You can write it the way you want it. Rewrite *your* story."

I took a deep breath. A sob escaped with my exhale.

My story, as tumultuous as it may have been, was mine. I couldn't always speak my truth; I was sometimes frozen, fearing my imaginings becoming reality. I often stopped short of what I wanted in order to allow another the chance to thrive. My words and retorts stuck in my throat and went stale on my tongue.

Then I'd put pen to paper. I created fiction from my reality, wove words into worlds, and breathed life into women forgotten. A little girl didn't live in fear within my pages. Not for long. The girl got the life she wanted. She said what she wanted. She lived in safety *with* her big, loud, and vibrant family. Her past could be troubled, tragic, *and* triumphant. She had no need to panic. Her backpack, full of doubts, fear, and panic, became the cape she wore in boardrooms, on stages, and while reading a book to her children.

Her story was now mine, too.

SHAY MICHELLE DRAPEAU

Shay Michelle Drapeau (CPCC, PVAA) started in documentary filmmaking and screenwriting 20 years ago. She is a writing coach and ghostwriter with her company, Mark It Done Virtual Solutions.

Driven by a deep-seated commitment to empowering women, Shay has recently added personal development coaching and advocacy for women's pursuit of their passions through her She Breathes Life™ brand to her coaching services. Her mission is to inspire, champion, and support women—regardless of their journey to that gender identity—in creative entrepreneurship through coaching, leadership, and community building.

Shay is all for a good audiobook performance and is ready for recommendations in Afrofuturism. Her writing is deeply inspired by romance, the books that shaped her as a teen, and the power of love in storytelling.

www.linkedin.com/in/sharondrapeau

www.instagram.com/sharondrapeau

www.instagram.com/shebreatheslife

www.facebook.com/shebreatheslife

www.sharondrapeau.com

www.shebreatheslife.com

7

UNEXPECTED HARMONY

JENNIFER HURLEY

My eyes bounce between the time on the phone screen perched to my left and the mirror in front of me. Leaning in and tilting my head toward the light, I focus on stilling the tremor in my hands as I rush to apply the last of my make-up. Ten minutes, and I still need to get from this concrete and cedar bathroom to the top of the field. Hundreds of people are waiting for me to start the show in a Texas Hill Country pasture with a brand-new, festival-sized stage. By brand new, I mean the carpenter finished putting the last screws in the ramp at 11:30 a.m.

We took just-in-time construction to an entirely new level for this one, I think, seeing my lips flicker into a brief grin in the mirror's reflection.

After seven minutes of frantic hand flapping with my cosmetics and wiggling my feet into rhinestone-covered boots, I am at the top of that ramp listening to David Abeyta tell me not to flinch when they start playing over my intro.

From behind me, I hear Ed Jurdi say to the band, "Get on my stage, motherfuckers."

The clock strikes 8 p.m. and six of us walk out to the cheering crowd. I lean into the mic, eyes sweeping the mass of humanity bathed in the burnished gold light of sunset, phone with my script forgotten in my hand.

How in the world did I pull this off? It's even better than I imagined. Who thought putting me up here was a good idea? Shoot, was that my idea? Wait, no. Freaking Jeska is to blame. Oh my god, say something. Now, c'mon, they are waiting!

"Welcome, everyone, to Jester King Brewery! I'm Jennifer Harlan, the Live Music Program Manager, and we have a fantastic line-up for you tonight! We are kicking off with Jamie Lin Wilson, then celebrating the return of The Band of Heathens to Austin! Are y'all ready? Alright! In that case, let's start this show!"

I beat what I hope looks like a strategic retreat from the stage, stepping over cords and instrument cases and pausing behind the back wall. I lean against the railings that still smell of sap and saw blades. My heart is a driving downbeat, drowning out the band's opening strains.

That's it. My job is done. Six months of insanity at the end of a six year journey, completed in sixty seconds of pure, unadulterated exhilaration and a sense of accomplishment.

My first coherent thought, strangely, is *What's next?* Followed almost immediately by my most common question: *How is this my life?*

People talk about needing to pinch themselves on occasion to believe they aren't living in a dream. Luckily, I'm clumsy enough not to need to actively harm myself, but otherwise, I count myself firmly in their camp. In many ways, my life is a collection of universal shenanigans, colliding stars of opportunity and preparation that solidify into a series of serendipitous occurrences like the one currently in progress around me.

My mind circles back to my thoughts onstage about my friend Jeska. She can certainly be considered the asteroid that struck my carefully constructed life, the catalyst to the conflagration that oriented my life around passion and pleasure instead of pain.

My belief in universal shenanigans was already well-established when Jeska came into my orbit and changed the trajectory of my life. I had spent my entire twenties as a "student of life," working full-time while taking academic classes and exploring my interests wherever they led. They led to many unique places that gave me a broad skill set, an appreciation for others, and a malleable sense of reality. Open-minded almost to a fault, I found myself in multiple situations where the best way out was through, earning all the wisdom that only mistakes and missed opportunities can teach you.

When Jeska found me, I was in the middle of one of the five recognized significant life events (birth, coming of age, marriage, divorce, or death), once again staring into a mirror while hands flapped about me with brushes and paint. This time, they were being wielded by a professional make-up artist who had driven three hours to be there. I had been stuck in the room for hours, first for hair and now for make-up. Without the aid of the vape pen the stylist brought in, I likely would have run screaming. I wouldn't have run away entirely; it was my shindig. But the voices of the other women in the room, combined with the copious amounts of hair products and perfumes, were overwhelming, and I was already nervous. My eyes stayed closed while the liner was applied, and I soaked in the darkness behind my eyelids, letting the sounds around me become background noise for a moment.

Of course, the moment couldn't last, and a few minutes later, I heard my sister say, "Hey Jenn, there's a woman outside who is here with the band and has a question for you."

"Tell her to come in here," I said, not bothering to crack my eyelids. "I'm not going anywhere for a bit." I laughed because it was an awesome day despite my momentary disassociation.

Leaning my head back so I wouldn't get stabbed in the eye by a mascara wand, I looked over as the door opened, and my sister walked back in, followed by a redhead straight from Irish central casting, complete with a perfectly fitted emerald green dress. Her hair was piled on top of her head, and she had pushed up the sunglasses, using them like a hairband. If it had been any other day, I would have felt insecure with her standing in front of me, composed and put together from head to toe. I had never made fashion look that effortless. I had actually seen her from across a crowded pub a couple of weeks prior and was aware of who she was, though we hadn't spoken.

"Hi, I'm Jeska. I'm here with Guy to help him set up to sing for the ceremony."

Guy Forsyth was the musician we had hired for the day, an almost-friend we had been fans of for a long time. It was one of the better ideas my partner had come up with, and I was thrilled.

"I know. It is so nice to meet you! I'm glad you are here, and you look gorgeous. Want some champagne? A snack? We have everything, and I don't think it will get eaten." My words sped up toward the end, my inner hostess coming to the forefront.

"Are you sure? I'm not trying to interrupt your day in any way, and congratulations on your wedding! Everything out there looks gorgeous. I would love to hang out and chat, but I need to go help finish setting up in a few minutes," she said, also speaking quickly. "I had something I wanted to do for you this evening, but I wanted to meet you and make sure it was okay. I know some people don't like surprises on their wedding day. Would it be okay for me to sing a song solo at the reception for you and your new husband?"

I nodded while my brain tried to find words to put together in an order that made sense. It might be my wedding day, but I had spent the previous six months planning this event with my 200 guests in mind, and people rarely give me unexpected gifts. I didn't even know this woman, and she didn't know me; the idea that she would want to do anything for a stranger did not compute.

"I would love that. Thank you very much." It was a simple reply but the best I could do in the moment. We spent a few more minutes talking, breaking the ice a bit before she had to head back out, and I was called to deal with one of the minor problems that made it past my coordinator and matron of honor.

Jeska came back a few times throughout the day. I learned she had recently moved to Austin from San Angelo, where she had run a club and booked live music. She followed Guy here to be with him and to further her music career. For someone whose personality reflected only Boss Babe energy, her body language and speech patterns betrayed her nervousness.

I understood why I was nervous. I was about to get up and say the vows I had finalized at about 8 a.m. that morning to a man I had known for over a decade in front of more people than I could keep straight. It had rained for a solid two and a half weeks, only stopping a couple of days prior. The entire staff at Jester King Brewery, where the wedding was being held, including their brewers and production team, had spent the previous two days laying mulch pathways and cleaning up the space. There may have been some panic on my part in the days leading up to this occasion, but I didn't understand why Jeska would be nervous. I brushed it off as none of my business and got to the crazy business of getting hitched.

The ceremony was beautiful, with an archway of trees behind us, an army of support in front of us, and a sense of humor to the whole thing that was delightful. We vowed to love and honor each other regardless of what life brought and that our decade-long friendship was and would always be at the core of our foundation. Someone finally brought me a beer after we took photos, and we headed inside for the reception, pausing for the photographer to snap a few shots of me chugging my drink while my new husband beamed at the camera, holding my bridal bouquet in the classic pose.

Dancing into the reception to "Love Me Like a Reptile" by Motorhead, I was caught up in the moment's atmosphere. Tiny fairy lights wound their way up the thick poles holding up the luxury open-air barn, and the smell of homemade tomato sauce and fresh dough from the wood-fired pizza truck outside spiced the air in a pleasing contrast to the floral decor arrayed around the space.

With toasts complete and plates full in front of us, the live music started. I had never arranged a performance before, and sharing this musician's music with my blended group of friends and family was a strange feeling. Guy Forsyth's songs held inherent and specific meaning in my heart. I felt vulnerable as well as seen to my soul as he sang "The Things That Matter," the complicated emotions of such a huge life change not far from the surface. Joy, fear, grief for the people I wished could have been there, excitement, anticipation, and more that I'm not even sure we have names for.

When it was Jeska's turn at the mic, no one would have thought she had only met me earlier that afternoon. She gave us a short toast, making the crowd laugh when she said that while she thought I was awesome, she could only assume that my husband was also cool by association. She apologized for having the lyrics in front of her, a habit that would take her years to stop doing. It was cute, and my first impression of her was set. She hadn't sung a note, and I was already a fan.

Guy began to play the opening notes of "Downpour" by Brandi Carlisle, and people visibly sat back when Jeska began to sing, her voice strikingly beautiful. Full and resonant, gone were any sign of the nerves I had seen earlier, her eyes closed as she sang about being the rain. The candlelight from the tables brought out the fire in her hair and the sparkle in her dress, and I knew I would always hold on to this memory once it was made. Life rarely matches the magic of a movie set, and I felt all five of my senses straining to take it all in.

My gratitude was overwhelming, blooming inside me
as she serenaded the room, creating a once-in-a-lifetime
memory for every person there. When she finished,
there was that oh-so-telling beat of silence before my
guests began to applaud and cheer, the one you could
find at the end of any great performance where the
crowd has to take a moment to come back to
themselves before they remember that they are
supposed to clap.

I may not have worked so hard to soak it in if I had
known how many more magic moments Jeska would
manifest for me. I continually find myself comparing her
to wildfires, hurricanes and other forces of nature
because words like kind, generous, and even larger than
life cannot convey the presence she exudes. The after-
effects of her random act of kindness were akin to
lightning striking damp sand in a storm, creating chaotic
art full of clarity, sparking fires that burned away the
undergrowth that enabled me to grow.

After returning from our honeymoon, I did not expect to
hear from Jeska. But I was pleasantly surprised to turn
my phone back on after two weeks in Mexico to several
text messages and an invitation to hang out. She had
already turned me into a big fan, so I had several
awkward moments reconciling that with our growing
friendship. I assumed that I was a convenient friend for a

girl who was new to town but was generally out of my league socially.

Jeska never saw me that way, and somewhere in year two of knowing each other, around the same time she kidnapped me for maternity pictures and then sat in my labor and delivery room for over twelve hours, earning the title of "The Only Person Other Than Medical Professionals to See My Internal Organs," it finally sunk in that this absolute badass warrior of a best friend considered me just as amazing as she was.

My daughter was born three weeks before the world shut down. Suddenly, I was a new mom, recovering from an emergency C-section and postpartum preeclampsia with a newborn. There were more than a few Tiger King episodes at 2 a.m. while breastfeeding and texting new parent questions to Jeska. She talked me off the ledge and off of Google, and, in general, did her best to keep me sane while navigating the sudden absence of live music anywhere in the world and having to replace her and her husband's income with zero notice.

One silver lining to that really tough time for the world was that Jeska and I started working together on the side. She was live-streaming house concerts of her and Guy playing about a week before anybody else figured it out, and I got to play chat moderator and occasional emcee. She hired me to make t-shirts for her to sell as I had gone full craft goblin at the time, and I was again impressed by her insistence on keeping the business stuff separate from our friendship. Previous attempts of mine to mix business with personal relationships had made me wary, so it was refreshing to have a simple transaction without any fuss.

A year into working from home with an infant either asleep on my desk or across the hall on my husband's, I hit a breaking point. I was a senior project manager for a fintech company, with all of the accomplishments and burnout you would expect from an undiagnosed ADHD-er in a fast-paced, high-stress environment for over seven years. I went to see my doctor, the one who had saved my life during childbirth the year before, and he told me he was about to have to do it again.

"Jenn, your stress levels are too high. You are going to have a stroke in the next six months if something doesn't change."

"But Doc, what can I do?"

"What's one thing you can do, today, to reduce your stress levels?"

"I guess, I guess I could go quit my job?"

"Yes. Go do that. Right now."

The story of how I quit my job and then landed my—at-the-time—dream job as an Innkeeper in three phone calls before I finished my drive home from the doctor's office is one that will have to wait. But a few weeks later, my daughter was in daycare, and I was the sole caretaker of a five-acre, twenty-bed Inn connected to Jester King Brewery and its one-hundred-and-sixty-acre ranch.

Jeska met me there a few days into it, and after I gave her the full tour, we settled on the lodge's central patio. Takeout coffees, three cell phones and a cigarette pack were scattered on the table in front of us. I had just wound down my info-dumping enough to ask her for her opinion on the place and ways to boost my marketing plan, which I had zero dollars to put behind.

"You know, that area right across from here in front of those three trees, you could put a small stage out here, have some ticketed concerts and bring in artists." She gestured toward the space she referenced, though I could picture it as soon as she said the words.

"Jes, I have literally no idea how to do that. I don't even know where to start," I almost whined, as I could feel my still-crispy burnt self starting to get excited and mentally begin piecing together what I knew I would need to pull it off.

"Start with the stage. Figure that out, and we can figure out the rest," she said, then proceeded to spend the next hour dreaming with me about all the things we could do with the space.

I have a great photo of her sitting on that tiny, 12'x12'x18" wooden stage that I talked the brewery's engineer into building for me that spring. She's sitting with her denim-covered legs crossed, looking up at the camera, with four blue-white lights shining up at her from the corners, while the tree above is draped in heavy shadow. I had kept my end of our agreement and figured out the stage.

Luckily she also kept hers, and between her contacts and industry knowledge and my computer skills and marketing background, we pulled together a solid eight week concert series. It made money, though the few hundred dollars we came in above break-even didn't directly affect the bottom line. For once, however, doing something for "exposure" made real money over time. I took a full speed crash course in music booking and venue management, both of which have worked out in my favor.

We did two more series over the next eighteen months, and the contacts I made through those artists just continued to produce opportunity after opportunity. Arranging multiple music videos, photoshoots, podcasts, and TV interviews for the Inn continued to pull me deeper into the creative orbit of Austin. Every week I was able to meet more amazing people with incredible stories and talent. The amount of joy that it brought me was a daily gift that renewed itself. I would spend hours after a concert trying to wind down and relive my favorite songs and moments in my mind. It was both fun and profitable, which have long been two of my favorite words.

The success I was having at work was an inverted reflection of what was happening in my personal life. Like many, many other couples, the strain of the pandemic was too much for my marriage. We were great parents to our daughter but not great partners to each other. Over time, we realized we were causing each other more harm than good and separated. The divorce was finalized about a year later. Inflation rose thirty percent seemingly overnight, and I threw myself into work, running the Inn and being part of the brewery's leadership team. I entered my Boss Babe era with a plethora of plates spinning simultaneously that could not be allowed to drop.

Jeska was going through her own struggles: Her ex-husband passed away from cancer, her tween daughter was grieving while going through puberty, a third brush with skin cancer, and online stalkers—all almost stacked on top of one another. We leaned on each other but would sometimes go weeks without laying eyes on each other. Once, I saw her kids more over the course of a weekend than I saw her. She was in town, insanely busy, and needed help getting the girls ready to leave on a trip.

Jeska finally rented out the loft at the Inn as her studio, which at least increased our odds of having face-to-face interactions. The days when she had recorded a new song were some of the best. We would restart each new recording at least seven times trying to listen to the lyrics.

Neither of us was truly capable of three to four minutes of silence. She would write or draw or sort jewelry while I did admin tasks on my computer, body-doubling at its finest. I learned a lot about the artistic process and got deep insights into who she was, and she got a front-row seat to the inner workings of my brain and how I run a business.

I went to her when the brewery approached me about booking their live music for them. The last person had left unexpectedly and neglected to book a band for that Saturday afternoon. It was Wednesday morning when I sent her the SOS text. She had me set up with someone in less than half an hour, and a one-time request for me to book music for the brewery very quickly turned into an offer to run the entire live music program. They had tried once to copy the ticketed concert idea from the Inn but weren't happy with their side's turnout. Looking back, she set me up to impress at multiple moments that have proven to have been crucial opportunities.

That twisted redhead of fate pointed me like an arrow toward this new endeavor, and the Universe got with the program, too. An employee needed some short-term housing so I had a free, onsite backup for the Inn and could dedicate those hours to the music program. My now ex-husband and I adjusted our custody schedule so there was less back and forth every week; our divorce was still freshly final, but the worst parts were behind us. Time, space and support to build this new adventure fell into place so gracefully that to an outside eye it might look like I had planned it. I very much did not, but I did take full advantage.

Shortly after I asked Jeska almost the same question I had before: How in the world do I turn a ranch into a concert venue? And (perhaps not) surprisingly, I got almost the same answer.

"You need a stage, babe. You have a giant field. You could rent four stages and have a festival out here if you wanted." When I told her my budget she reined in her dreams a bit. Still, that immediate, unwavering confidence in not just the space itself but in my ability to pull it together was...well, "impactful" feels inadequate as a description.

Exactly ninety days after the day the leadership team agreed to let me launch the program, I had my first show, with just shy of 800 guests. For those not familiar with the industry, that short timeline, for that size of a show doesn't happen when you are starting from scratch, building relationships with agencies and artists, and having to phone a friend to double-check you are using the right terms with people and don't sound like a noob. That the show happened on a fully-built (minus the ramp), festival-sized stage that hadn't existed two weeks beforehand probably had the same odds as winning the Powerball. Those odds, when you add in randomly meeting the other band I was targeting to come play while on a plane home from Ft. Lauderdale, and then their support getting both concert deals over the finish line...well, you either call in a mathematician or accept that it's divine interference.

Jeska, with her band, the Vanity Project, opened for me before Shinyribs that first show night, for which my only regret is her calling me out from the stage as "the reason any of this is happening" while physically pointing me out to the crowd. God love the woman. I had been out there for twelve hours already, and my feet were killing me, but the show must go on. And it did, with Jeska shimmering in her dress of oversized gold sequins.

Watching her captivate an audience on the stage I had built, our talents and efforts combined, I couldn't help but connect back to that first moment watching her sparkle under the lights, her voice raised as my soul changed pitch and found its harmony. The memory lives rent-free in my head, often playing on repeat when I am uncertain of my next steps.

Coming back to that heart of gratitude and conversations with my personal burning bush always seems to clear the path. Jeska is an unstoppable force, loving people and life with abandon.

The last verse of "Downpour" that she sang on the eve of our fateful meeting has become almost an accidental vow between us.

"I'm going to be there for you" is the silent, unconscious melody that plays beneath our every interaction, like Lamb Chop's "Song That Doesn't End." It just goes on and on, this heartwarming duet with my friend.

JENNIFER HURLEY

Jennifer Hurley, PMP, is an Austin-based writer and entrepreneur who specializes in true stories of serendipity or "Universal Shenanigans." A lifelong passion for poetry, combined with her unique perspective on life has laid the foundation for her unique narrative voice.

Jennifer owns Rhythm Road Entertainment, a creative agency set to launch in October 2024, which blends her love for live music with curating unforgettable experiences for others.

Even with the demands of her business, a young child, a soon-to-be spouse and a puppy, Jennifer still manages to invite readers to join her on a journey where the unexpected becomes the extraordinary.

Find out more about her life and current projects, including links to her podcast, at www.RhythmRoad.co

8

FROM CRISIS TO CLARITY

SUSIE MOCERI

---

*O*ctober 21, 2020

The morning after my middle daughter's eighth birthday, I returned home from dropping off my four kiddos at school. I plopped down at the desk in my home office, placing a cup of tea next to my laptop, eager to respond to the daily prompts from my *Clarity with Carrie* course. My heart sat in a warm and fuzzy space, appreciative of my personal growth over the past year. With hands poised over the keyboard, my phone buzzed beside me with a Facebook Messenger notification.

You should know your husband has been cheating on you for many years with many young women.

I felt the all-too-familiar crack of my life breaking apart.

Again.

An involuntary shakiness began in my fingers and hands as my eyes passed over those lines repeatedly, and a thrumming coursed through my body. Several moments —perhaps minutes—passed while I felt on the cusp of unraveling, as I had done two and a half years earlier when a similar incident occurred.

However, this time, I had Carrie—a woman who had entered my life earlier that year. I realized my work with her had prepared me to face this life-shattering moment with strength and clarity. And I knew what I had to do.

* * *

March 22, 2018

The day after my niece was born, I picked up Taco Deli for my brother, his wife, and my mom on the way to the hospital. I couldn't wait to hold this tiny newborn and congratulate my brother. Having lived states apart for decades, I could never have predicted that he and I would live in the same town, let alone have children six months apart.

It should have been a joyful and celebratory day, but it quickly became one of the defining moments of my life.

In the midst of perhaps his proudest moment, my brother caught my eye and, with a determined voice with a slight hitch in it, said, "Hey, Suz, can I chat with you in the hallway?"

My heart dropped, and my body buzzed with my intuition's anticipation of bad news.

"Where's [your husband]?" he asked after the door shut behind us in the hallway.

"He's been in Dallas for work," I replied.

My brother looked at me with discomfort as he said, "No, he's not. He's here in Austin."

My mind was slow to pick up on what he told me, but my body instinctively knew. I tensed as the words I expected came next.

"He was with a girl last night. She reached out to me on Facebook. I'm so sorry to tell you, but he's been cheating on you."

The rest of the conversation was a blur. We returned to the room with his wife holding his baby girl and my mom enjoying the tacos. I allowed myself a few minutes with a fake smile plastered on my face while my heart crumbled inside before excusing myself. As I stuttered out of the room and through the labyrinth of halls, my lungs took short, erratic breaths. I tried focusing on maintaining my composure as I exited the hospital. When I reached my parked car in the garage, I could no longer hold back the tears that had been blurring my vision, and they streamed down my face as I screamed and pounded my steering wheel.

That evening, I confronted my husband. Although he initially denied any wrongdoing, he quickly realized I had enough proof and nothing he could say would convince me otherwise. I summarily told him to get out of the house.

I barely ate one meal a day and could only succumb to a couple of hours of sleep, all while having a six-month-old in our family of (now) six. The only thing that got me through that time were my meetings with my therapist, varying between one to three times per week— sometimes just to have an excuse to get out of bed.

I told my therapist that I wasn't suicidal. But, I craved being unconscious—a mini reprieve from reality, not desiring anything permanent, but simply escaping the pain in my heart, the spiraling feeling of being out of control, and the inevitable need to make decisions and move forward.

Meanwhile, I was also frantically trying to gather information from the girls (yes, I discovered multiple) who had contacted me, which was my attempt to grasp a sense of control in my life, desperately seeking to know all the sordid details and gather proof in case I decided to pursue a divorce. But each new day dropped a hail of bombs, shocking and devastating information in texts and Facebook messages—details no wife should ever hear from a young side piece—which flung me into paralyzing depths of despair and hopelessness.

When one sent me screenshots of their conversations, I compared the timestamps of messages my husband had sent her against the ones he had sent me. I realized he was setting up a tryst with her, and the next minute, he sent me a message asking what was for dinner. It felt like the entirety of my reality glitched. Another time, he texted me while he was out of town and said he was going to take an Ambien and head to bed. However, the reality was that he was actually in town but with a girl, sending me a requisite good-night text that would cease any further conversation with me that night.

And there was the rage.

Yes, a rage that was unknown to me before. A searing, seething electricity that burned through my veins. The "fight" instinct overcame my body. One night, I pummeled his chest and back with my palms and my fists. I was appalled and frightened the next day when my knuckles were bruised and hurt. While I didn't harm him, as he is almost a foot taller and eighty pounds heavier, I am not a violent person, and this uncontrollable, visceral, animal, snarling fury was unfamiliar and scary.

During the months immediately following that initial revelation of his behavior, I may have smashed a bottle of wine when he refused to answer my questions. I may have screamed at him outside our home, with him urging me to be quiet while I dared him to push me further, not caring in the moment if and what the neighbors heard. I may have threatened to destroy his laptop, ready to throw it over a retaining wall in the driveway to the street below—this holy housing of all his work and also the hub of his behavior that destroyed our marriage. I may have forced my way into the casita, where he had taken to sleeping, shoving the dresser he had barricaded in front of the door out of the way to compel him to answer my questions.

Not my finest hours.

My husband and I had dated for six years on and off until we finally decided to get married. While there were a couple of episodes of questioning if he was cheating on me, he would inevitably return to me, begging me to give him another chance, claiming he only wanted to be with me. It was the hubris of being a girl in my twenties who believed his committing to marriage to me indicated he was choosing monogamy with me. I foolishly believed I was intelligent and beautiful enough to keep his attention on me.

Thirteen years of marriage and four children later, with the life we had created together, confronting the fact he was never the monogamous man I thought he was made my pain that much more intensely concentrated.

The entire lens through which I viewed the world had been shattered. I wandered through a foggy existence, where my brain wanted to shut down to cocoon myself in a space of emptiness to the point where I became scared, acknowledging it was dangerous to drive while being distracted and disconnected.

Then I had the joyful experience of patches of scaly skin appear on my face and legs. I had never had skin issues before, and when I went to see a dermatologist, the biopsy returned with a diagnosis of psoriasis, an autoimmune disease that decided to rear its ugly head during this time of crisis. Perfect—when I felt most rejected and undesirable, now this. My body was screaming from the stress, literally exploding and expressing it physically. After several months, it disappeared and has not since returned.

I felt powerless in my life as I considered our four young children and how everything he had done and how we would now proceed would affect them. I felt embarrassed by my ignorance, yet in the center of that dwelled a kernel of appreciation for my intuition. Because I knew all along that something was not right, despite his efforts to gaslight and manipulate me.

There were frequent "business dinners" that turned out to be with a female "associate" that ran late into the night, with expensive receipts for restaurants and bars. When I questioned him about them, I was met with defensiveness and excuses, and inevitably, he shifted the blame onto me for snooping. However, soon afterward, his wallet held thousands of dollars in cash instead of receipts.

He had learned to adapt.

I was not proud to admit that I searched his wallet. But when enough red flags were raised, some investigation was warranted. There was the unfamiliar pair of women's panties I found years before in the laundry. My heart pounded as I realized they weren't mine, and my mind raced through various scenarios of how they ended up in my laundry bin, but then it was like a switch flicked in my brain as I quickly—almost on autopilot— shoved them halfway down in the trash and promptly swiped the occurrence out of my mind, choosing not to dwell on it, quickly opting for denial instead. If I ignored it, it didn't happen.

Once the proof became undeniable, I felt disgusted and humiliated to discover that several (who knows how many) people not only knew all about his disregard for our marriage but were complicit in hiding his behavior—facilitating payments and drafting NDAs. It was like an inner web of dirty men who, because they were on his payroll, kowtowed to his secret life. Men who may very well be participants in these indiscretions, cheating on their wives. Men who I have welcomed into my home, cooked for, entertained, and hosted—given of myself.

Three months into that initial crisis period, we found a marriage counselor who helped me articulate that I would be willing to work on our marriage if it meant we would emerge better than before. Clearly, some problems needed to be addressed, but, bottom line, I didn't want to divorce. *If* we could improve our communication and interactions, I would prefer to save the marriage—for our children's sake primarily, but also for my own. That dangling hope for a *better* relationship opened the door for optimism. His alleged desire to save the marriage offered a glimmer of hope that it could be possible.

I'll be honest: in addition to the devastating pain and heartbreak that accompanied feeling rejected and undesirable, I also felt incredibly fearful about what my future would be if we divorced. I had been a stay-at-home mom, out of the professional sphere for many years. Questions swirled in my mind about how I would support myself financially, dreading the thought of giving up the privileged lifestyle I had become accustomed to having.

What kind of job could I acquire that would offer this lifestyle? Before marriage, I earned the modest salary of a high school English teacher. What if I had to move into a tiny apartment and accept a mediocre job that made me unavailable to my children?

Furthermore, what man would be attracted to a woman in her mid-forties who has four young children, whose body bears the scars and wear that accompany pregnancy, labor, and age—whose own husband had zero sexual interest in her? What if I never found the kind of man who would treat me how I desired? What if I aged lonely and died alone?

What if my kids would blame and hate me for breaking up the family?

Our marriage counselor assigned us homework to write a letter to each other.

Holy hell, I easily unleashed a ten-page manifesto that bared my broken soul and questioned him on every detail.

I was desperate and eager to communicate my pain, questions, and fears through my writing, which has always been an easier method of communication. I clarified what I wanted to say and took the time to do so with deliberation. I needed to know that he understood how severely he had hurt me.

Since I was the one who was affronted, during the next session, I was shocked, disappointed, and—quite frankly —angry when the marriage counselor insisted my husband share his letter first.

When he read his letter, I could hardly believe what I heard. He explained that "every red-blooded American male entering middle age innately desires these same things, and [he] just had the means and motivation to carry through on some of these natural feelings." He further defended his actions as a natural byproduct of middle age, "rebelling against the habitual conventions and routines of family life." He also admitted "that the desire for the excitement of those illicit activities will not simply disappear overnight—it would be almost unnatural for them to somehow dissipate on their own."

What stood out most in the moment—and has stayed with me to today—was his admission that "the guilt and sadness I feel right now is derived from the pain I've caused you rather than the actions underlying them."

Whoa, hold on.

Wait, what?

WHAT? Are you *fucking* kidding me!

Did I hear that correctly?

I asked him for a hard copy of his letter, and indeed, that is precisely what he had written. His momentary honesty and emotional awareness stunned me, for he rarely approached anything that might cause conflict and share his raw truth.

But his truth differed immensely from mine; I didn't know how to bridge that gap. He shared that his guilt lay in causing me pain, but he didn't feel remorse or shame for his actual transgressions. That incongruence of values was something I quietly sensed in that moment would likely not lead to a flourishing, improved marriage, despite my deep desire to salvage our relationship and his claim that he wanted the same.

* * *

January 2020

Nearly two years after discovering my husband's infidelities, we had settled into a status quo of relative peace. Occasional outbursts still punctuated the scene when familiar feelings of doubt, insecurity, and distrust bubbled up. But, for the most part, by this point, we had moved through the crisis phase, during which I had alternated between periods of grief and wailing, to rage and destruction, to hibernation and retreat.

We had just purchased a beautiful house a few months prior and hired an interior designer. I worked side-by-side with her to decorate and renovate everything: choosing every paint color, carpet and flooring, lighting fixtures and chandeliers, backsplashes, countertops, furniture, and artwork. It represented an opportunity to change the scenery of our lives and begin afresh. I dove into the project and stupidly thought he wanted or allowed me to take the lead. In hindsight, he very likely was relieved that I had a distraction.

Because his behavior, as I would soon learn, had never changed.

Meanwhile, my children's school advertised a parenting workshop with a guest speaker. Even long before becoming a mother, I sought to learn about parenting and early childhood development. My vocation was working with high school students, but when I became pregnant for the first time, I knew there was so much more I wanted to learn about those early developmental stages.

The Head of School introduced Carrie Contey, Ph.D, and she immediately drew me in. This woman took to the podium with her shoulder-length, black curly hair with some white peppered throughout—somehow wild yet tamed and absolutely beautiful. When she opened her mouth and began talking, her passion for her work became clear and magnetic, and she had a captivating smile and an energy that enlivened me.

She shared a new-to-me parenting paradigm: we have shifted from the dictatorial manner of how we were raised to seeing and appreciating these little humans gifted to us. Rather than the "blank slates" who are born to parents whose responsibility is to discipline misbehavior and lead them toward excellence, they already arrive as a whole little person whose parents' primary responsibility (other than to provide basic needs) is to guide them through their development and help them learn to regulate their emotions.

She talked about the different Brain States that humans have: Reptilian, Mammalian, and Human, and how beneficial it is to recognize when we exist within each state, when we need to back up, take a break, get resourced, or thrive when we are in our highest, most regulated Human state.

As Carrie spoke, I knew that I wanted more. I found I sat up straighter, nodding my head throughout her presentation.

After she finished, I didn't want this experience or interaction to end. I felt compelled to approach her, something I would never usually do. But for some reason, I did.

I said, "I love and am fascinated by what you have shared today, but I have four littles. It's... different. Do you have any advice for someone with a larger family?"

She acknowledged that parenting four children is a wholly different beast. We chatted briefly, and she invited me to join her email list, which I did. I left the room feeling lighter and optimistic that I had learned some parenting tools that would help me. In particular, I understood the "power of the pause" when a kiddo's outburst would trigger my temper. Inevitably, we would be flung into our Reptilian brain state, where nothing productive could emerge. Being able to pause, name, and tame emotional swirls, catching yourself before acting makes sense, but it can be so challenging when caught up in the emotions. I consciously and intentionally began to be aware of when I would get dysregulated.

After signing up to be on Carrie's email list, I received a "Carrie's Notes" email from her every few weeks. In them, she provided encouragement, awe, appreciation, and inspiration as we were all muddling our way through the pandemic, reminding us to keep in mind that "Presence over perfection"—with ourselves and with our others—is the goal.

Another gem was:

We're not who we were.

We are who we are.

And that's always and ever-evolving.

(Most especially in the midst of quarantine.)

As you keep unfolding...

Feel the feelings.

Weather the weather.

Dream the dreams.

Allow the growth.

Be wide open to newness.

Trust yourself.

Trust your people.

Appreciate it all.

and

Choose love!

Additional reminders to be tuned into our energy, feel alignment within ourselves, and do the things to nourish and regulate ourselves had nestled and started to take root in my mind. In August of 2020, Carrie offered a *Fall Clarity for All*, a three-hour Zoom workshop to settle, tune in, and journal to prepare for the transition into the fall season. I participated in that mini-retreat, which was illuminating and resourceful. I jumped at the opportunity when Carrie introduced her offering for a nine-month *Clarity* course. It would include daily emails with writing prompts, weekly Zoom meetings to meet and write with the group, and monthly one-on-one phone calls with Carrie.

During my introductory call with Carrie, I asked her if she intentionally created the course to cover nine months, representing a gestational period to me. She acknowledged it was meant to last the duration of the school year, but I shared with her that I viewed it as a sign: after having gestated four little humans, this course was a timely opportunity to focus on myself, to gestate myself into the next phase. I had no idea what the foreshadowing of that statement held nor how powerful an influence Carrie would have in the ensuing months and years.

Through abundant work with my therapist and Carrie, I uncovered and named the "Goddess Warrior" within me. When Carrie's writing prompt asked, "What is Clarity for me," my journaled response was, "Clarity is the Goddess Warrior's Knowledge, Truth, and Power being acknowledged and accepted by my consciousness or Thinking Brain. It is the peace that arises out of aligning the Head, Heart, and Gut. These lightbulb moments, the 'Ah-ha's,' can then allow formulating a plan, a direction, a purpose. It feels peaceful and soothing. It feels empowering and liberating. It feels exciting and anticipatory. It feels like an acceptance of Truth. It feels like a synchronicity of the individual with the Universe."

Through responding to Carrie's writing prompts, I discovered that the stress I experience when faced with an external event (person, activity, or news) results from confronting an imbalance or disruption of that reality against my Gut Brain, my Essence, the Goddess Warrior. At first, I viewed the Goddess Warrior as a separate part of myself that had been quieted, abandoned, and ignored. As I started to lean into her wisdom, I anticipated the day she would swell and inhabit a more prominent space within me until she would be me and I would be her.

***

October 21, 2020

I didn't crumble into a puddle when that fateful day's Facebook Messenger notification appeared. I was finally fortified to meet it with clarity. I knew, within my core—despite all my efforts to make the marriage work—I could not nor would not accept less than what I deserved.

When I looked back on my recent journaling about insights I had gained about my inner strength, a calm washed over me.

It was actually relief.

Giving up my hope that this marriage would improve was a relief. Yes, there was an incredulous anger at what he had continued to do—the lies, betrayal, and rejection. I was angry that I had given him another chance. I was furious that he had definitively destroyed my dream of a happy, loving, life-long marriage with him.

I felt anxiety about what lay ahead and grief for the years-long decay and dissolution of our marriage.

But anxiety is love holding its breath. I had been living with shallow breathing and white-knuckling through the future's uncertainties.

I was finally clear that I was done.

And it felt liberating.

I sat up straight in my chair and drafted an email to my attorney, writing I had discovered his continued infidelity and instructed her to file for divorce immediately. My pinky hovered over the "Enter" button while I took a few shaky breaths. But when I firmly clicked on it, I inhaled deeply, followed by an extended exhale. I gradually released the questions, doubts, and fears that had gripped me for the past several years about whether my marriage would survive. And with each slow inhale and exhale, my focus shifted from the past to the future, on moving through this next phase with as much civility, dignity, and grace as I could muster.

I didn't have to settle.

I didn't have to feel trapped.

I could dictate how my future would unfold.

* * *

After my ex-husband was served with the divorce papers, there was a time when he again begged me to reconsider. He expressed his surprise at how calm and determined I was—no surprise after the tumultuous period we had lived through a couple of years prior. But I had become a different person by then.

Continued conversations with Carrie helped me clarify that I wanted to move through the divorce process with as much grace and civility as possible. Despite receiving legal advice to go to war with him, I knew that was not in service to me or my children. I ultimately negotiated a settlement agreement on my own, *without* going to war, that I could accept with peace and—quite frankly —celebration.

Next, we decided to "nest," meaning the children would stay in the house while my ex and I would have separate domiciles, taking turns at the house. This scenario would be the least disruptive for my four kiddos. Once I realized this meant I would have a separate space, a new realm of possibility unfolded.

Carrie introduced the exercises of "dream writing" and "future writing," where you put pen to paper and express the best possible scenario you can imagine. A similar exercise she shared was "What if up-ping." When stressed, people tend to "What if–down," allowing their thoughts to swirl downward into potential worst-case scenarios. The first time I participated in responding to that prompt, it was easy to vomit my negative thoughts onto the page. Reviewing prior journal entries showed how naturally and quickly my thoughts spiraled downward.

The next step is to consider "What if—neutral," which often looks like an acceptance of "It is what it is." The final step is to "What if—up" and allow your mind to open up to the best possible outcomes or dreams come true.

I always viewed myself as an "optimistic realist," meaning I know our time here will include both good and bad and that we will inevitably experience a whole range of adverse events, but underneath it all, I believe things will turn out well. However, I often kept my dreams quiet because expressing my deepest desires to the Universe was vulnerable. I feared failing to accomplish them.

I learned from my work with Carrie that the potential feelings of disappointment or failure should not outweigh putting forth positive thinking and energy; those vibrations can often attract precisely what you desire, "Energy follows intention."

When I considered and journaled about my separate living space, I described something luxe, feminine, and did not worry about having the furnishings suitable for children. I toured a few condos downtown but was most eager about the last one on my list. The real estate agent opened the unit's door, and the curved floor-to-ceiling windows revealed a bright unit with stunning panoramic views. It held an exquisite finish-out, wallpapered accent walls, silk valances and drapes, sparkling crystal embellishments and chandeliers, and feminine artwork. I was filled with joy because it was a moment where I felt like the universe dropped this gift into my lap—the perfect space for me at the ideal time. It surpassed what I envisioned in luxury, and I was stunned and grateful.

One prompt Carrie sent about a year after I filed for divorce asked, "What bits of wisdom are you gathering about yourself lately?" My response reveals how my work with her was already affecting a shift in my mindset:

"Look up" is a phrase that resonates with me because I find that I tend to look down— literally and figuratively. Dealing with the four children, I'm physically looking down at them, at the toys, disarray, and crumbs on the floor. When I take my dog for walks, I look down at the ground to watch where I'm walking to avoid stepping on other dogs' poops, ant piles, or snakes. Of course, when I'm looking at my phone to check social media, read the news, or play games, I'm looking down.

All that looking down causes my shoulders to hunch forward, and I slouch, creating extra tension in my body.

I'm reminding myself to look up, way up to the sky. I pull my shoulders back and stand up straighter, tilting my head back and opening my chest. I can immediately feel a little stronger in spirit and more open and welcoming to people and ideas.

I also tend to look down figuratively. Even when complimented, I interpret it negatively. My therapist says I'm "a wizard" at manipulating anything in a way that becomes critical of myself.

Building on a practice of appreciation and continuing to work on myself, I am noticing a tiny emergence of shifting toward looking up in my thoughts. So that's a new mantra that keeps presenting itself.

Look up.

Look up.

Look up...

Just the other day, during a Zoom meeting with Carrie and some other clients of hers, we did the "What if" exercise. After we finished writing, I joyfully shared with the group that my default of swirling down with my thoughts had shifted to "What if up-ping." This mindset has permitted my thinking to dream big, and I have experienced other dream-come-true moments.

During that first one-on-one call with Carrie, she asked me what dreams I had, and I shared my very quiet, guarded desire to become a published author. After years of journaling, writing for myself, and participating in writing workshops—with Carrie's guidance through dream writing—the Universe again presented me with an opportunity to meet with a local publisher, resulting in my getting published in a multi-authored book last year. Besides becoming a mother, this goal was my deepest, secret desire, and I was overjoyed when I finally held that book with my name on the cover.

Time marches on, and undoubtedly, I will face many more challenges, even crises, ahead. However, I am finally confident that I am strong enough to face whatever may come. My ex and I have forged a favorable co-parenting situation where we can celebrate all the special moments and go on family vacations together. He is a better, more present father now than he ever was before. And we are likely better co-parents than spouses. Now, he proposes investment opportunities as partners, whereas we needed more partnership in so many ways during our marriage.

Gone is the critical internal voice telling me *I am ugly, stupid, incompetent, undesirable, unlovable, and unworthy*. Instead, the Goddess Warrior remains, reminding me to appreciate and be intentional, celebratory, and playful.

She whispers, "You are enough. You are more than enough."

She urges me to listen to my intuition.

Dream big. And...

Look up.

SUSIE MOCERI

Susie Moceri discovered her passion for writing and reading at a young age and has been honing her craft ever since. With a BA in English and an M.Ed from the University of Florida, Susie explores themes of race, identity, love, and the complexities of the human experience in her writing.

After college, Susie pursued her childhood vocational dream in the classroom, dedicated to guiding and inspiring eleventh and twelfth grade students, fostering critical thinking, analytical writing, and a deep appreciation for literature.

Last year, Susie contributed her chapter entitled "Excavating the Goddess Warrior: A Journey Back to Myself" in the book *Going Places: Soul-Stirring Essays About The Travel That Changed Us*.

When not immersed in the world of words, Susie is busy raising her four children, being active in their school community and philanthropy, and making time to play with her Yorkie puppy.

www.facebook.com/susie.estabrook
www.instagram.com/estabrooksusie

9

FINDING SOUL PURPOSE

NATASHA ZIKE

I t was such a heartbreaking, unbelievable shock when my husband called me home from a neighbor's house to give me the news. He wouldn't tell me why he needed me home; he just said I needed to be there in person.

"Do you want me to tell you what it is, or do you want to read it?" he asked seriously.

How am I supposed to know? I don't even know what topic this is about!

"Sure, why don't you go ahead and tell me," I said.

A week and a half after that fateful day, I was preparing to sing a familiar song, in a familiar setting, after a tragic event, at one of the most stressful times of my life, at the service of one of my dearest friends.

I've performed "Because He Lives" at least twenty, maybe thirty times in my life so far, always at a funeral service of someone close, someone I loved, starting with my papaw's service when I was eleven.

Travis and I dated briefly almost two decades ago, and afterward, we became close, yet unexpected friends. He was loud and opinionated, the life of the party, the Dell technical trainer, the chef, the BBQ connoisseur, and the community builder. He was fiercely loyal to his country, to Texas, to our service members, to his beliefs, to helping his friends, to Texas A&M University, and he unequivocally loved his wife, Jina.

The loud and opinionated part of his personality could be polarizing. Sometimes, I'd have to tell him, "Travis, I love you, but I had to block you on social media again." There were times we just didn't see eye to eye on politics, religion, rights granted, or rights withheld, but if you sat this well-informed man down for a talk, he would listen to every word you had to say and try to understand your perspective, even if he disagreed. He was full of respect and deep care, and I loved him dearly. It turns out, just like Matthew McConaughey said after the Uvalde shooting, we are far more alike than we are different.

I was in shock and denial, and I couldn't even begin to

believe Travis was gone. Two weeks earlier, he had celebrated his fiftieth birthday.

I called his wife immediately. As it rang, I wondered if I was calling too soon, if it were true, but this was different. I couldn't rely on social media that might take days. I needed to know right then and there.

The phone rang twice. Jina answered.

No hellos. I start quietly, barely choking the words as I tried to speak. "Jina, tell me it isn't true."

Pause. "It's true, Tash. We lost him."

Travis's father had passed only a few months earlier, and Travis had been visiting his ailing mother for a few days to help take care of her. He went to sleep, and his mom couldn't wake him.

I vowed to help Jina with the service, as this was a familiar stomping ground for me.

We decided I would sing my song, my funeral song, for Travis. It was an honor. I could do my small part for him and his loved ones.

As you would expect, I had a lot going through my mind on the day of the service. But it wasn't just this devastating loss. My life outside the funeral was just as tumultuous and uneasy.

My husband and I had each worked at our beloved technology company for six years when they announced plans for another company to acquire it, and with that, the pending potential of a layoff. The crippling uncertainty of possibly losing our careers was compounded by the crushing sadness from losing Travis.

A few minutes before the service, I took Jina to the restroom to walk around and ease our nerves. It was a single-stall restroom, and I waited outside in the hallway.

Four minutes. Okay, I barely have just enough time to use the restroom and return to my seat. Gotta be quick. What's that text message from John?

Oh no...oh gosh...it's finally happened.

"Well, family, I just got my separation agreement from the company. It's official. I'm being laid off," my husband texted his family.

What does that mean for me? Did I lose mine, too?

Should I check my emails or not?

Can I go through the whole service without knowing whether I was also laid off?

I wanted to be present for this service.

My finger hovered over the button to find out...

Have you ever looked back at those big, pivotal moments or "forks in the road" on your life's path? I've noticed that we tend to see them only in hindsight, but in the moment, we often can't fathom just how big of a moment it will be in our life's journey.

Think of those decisions in your late teens and twenties —where you'll live, the people you'll befriend, the jobs you'll choose. Each one is a big decision at the moment. Then, a decade or two later, you look back, and BOOM, your life went in a fantastic direction all because of one small decision you made long ago. All in hindsight, though. Not usually seen in the future.

Last year, it was different for me. I knew that a big fork in the road was just on the horizon.

From start to finish, it would be almost eighteen months from the announcement to the acquisition. We didn't know when, or even if, it would happen, and we kept thinking the end was right around the corner, any day now, for months and months on end. It was frantic at times, especially as we assumed more and more responsibilities as people left, feeling pulled and pushed and tugged by the emotions of uncertainty. I needed to decide what I wanted to do with my life if I were laid off, and this seemed like the right time to plan it.

Thinking through the possibilities, fears in the form of questions swirled through my mind.

Will I be let go? If I'm still here, what kind of work will I do?

What about my husband?

If we are both let go, how long can we financially make it? How long can we survive?

Do we even want an offer to stay?

I was the Global Director of Learning and Development for a few major product lines, developing product training and certifications for our 40,000 employees and hundreds of thousands of companies and individuals. In addition to my day job, I also led a global Employee Resource Group with 1,200 members in thirty countries and a leadership staff of about one hundred.

My ERG leaders and I worked tirelessly to help our employees cope with the stress of the pending acquisition and prepare for their future. I hired external trainers to lead workshops on various subjects, including navigating change, understanding and utilizing their strengths, psychological safety, career progression and personal development, belonging, and bringing your whole self to work, on topics like using generative AI in resume writing, job searches, and applications, and finally, the one that made the most significant impact for me, a session on finding one's purpose.

I met Coach K (they/she) two months before the acquisition at a conference where they spoke. The slim, athletically built person on stage was dressed sharply in a striking white collared button-down shirt, a blue blazer, and blue jeans—casual yet professional. She was so handsome! The sides of her head were shaved with cool designs, and the rest of her black hair was in either dreads or tiny ringlets, I couldn't tell. She commanded the audience, which was silently watching.

"We have to ask ourselves, 'Who am I? What are my core values?" Coach K urged from the stage. "What are your gifts, and how do you use them to make an impact? What challenges have you overcome that you can walk others through? **What makes your life worth living?"**

Well, that was deep. I just sat down, lady!

She said people who live with purpose live longer.

I want to live a long, happy life, I thought.

She very purposefully said, "I'd like you to close your eyes and imagine you're 100 years old."

Remember, I'm practically sitting in front of her.

"We're walking into a party with all your loved ones at the end of your life. They are so excited to see you and celebrate this momentous occasion. Look around. Who's there? What have you done that they are celebrating? What achievements are you most proud to have accomplished?"

After we had spent some time on this exercise, and it had time to sink in, she asked us to tear a small piece of paper from our notepad and write down our job titles.

"Now rip them up and throw them in the middle of the table. These titles aren't your *essence*. They're a part of your mission. They're just the activities we complete but not who we are."

Lastly, she had us write down the span of our life with a dash between the numbers and two question marks for the end years.

I wrote: 1984 - 20??

I wondered what secrets those question marks hide.

"I want you to focus on the dash, she said from the stage "Every single thing you have ever and will ever do, every person you'll ever meet, every place you'll ever visit, everything you've owned or touched, and every person you've impacted exists within this dash between your birth and death. Make it a good dash, a dash worth living."

Boom.

By the end of her hour-long workshop, I had written down my entire life's purpose. Yes, you read that right. She had taken me and 200 other leaders at these well-known, major companies through a transformation, and I was bawling silently at a table of strangers doing the same.

Coach K had us start with our Core Values, and we whittled the large list down into specifics. My life's purpose formed:

"My purpose is to passionately create and live a life that brings joy, knowledge, strength, and purpose to all I encounter, connecting with, loving, and lifting others up along the way. Leaving this life a better place than when I found it."

I've thought of my purpose before, but never with such intensity and structure as in those forty-five minutes. Thank goodness I didn't miss it! It was such a transformative experience. I had to hire her as a speaker for our PRIDE month, which was now only two months away.

As we met to customize her content for my audience, the acquisition announcement had just occurred, and we added her resilience training to help folks who were starting to tailspin. I felt it was an urgent call for our employees to understand their distinct purpose in the world.

Wait a minute. This is for more than the employees I serve.

This training is for me, too. What will I do if I don't make the cut?

The purpose I distilled for myself in her workshop was that I need to use my strengths and lessons learned to guide others, making this world a better place than I found it, on as broad of a scale as possible. This call has always been my *essence*, but my actions or missions were really to find a way up and out of the circumstances I was born into as quickly as possible.

You see, I would have joined the foster care system if it weren't for my grandparents. I was the first in my family to go to college, and from my perspective, I was also the first to work, though my papaw had retired long before I was born from twenty years in the United States Army. We had very little money to support us, and I helped him collect cans out of dumpsters as a kid to get $100 a trash bag from the recycling center that paid for our food. He and my grandma were loving, and I owe them the world. I immediately cried writing that. I am beyond thankful and grateful for the intangible gifts they gave me when they took me in as a two-month-old baby. We may not have had a lot of money, but we sure had love.

By high school, I joined a church attended by wealthy kids, and I saw such different lives. It opened a new range of possibilities for my future in my head. I knew I was smart enough, and I could do what they did. I joined their clubs and had the fearlessness and self-confidence to go after really incredible jobs just because they sounded interesting.

I was a radio DJ at sixteen for a classic rock station. As a senior in high school, I continued working at the radio station, and I also worked behind the scenes of a local television news station, conducting cameras and adding live graphics to the broadcast. In college, I lent my voice to the university's radio station and made money by floor directing at another television news station.

Baylor is where I took a significant fork in the road. I chased a lead I overheard in the hallway about working for Dell Computers. As a freshman in college at nineteen, I started working for their giant corporation, trading television and radio for technology for the next twenty years. In my deep psyche, the goals were twofold:

I just don't want to be my mother. Anything I could do to avoid turning out like her was my goal. What a motivating factor that was. I loved her, but I unfortunately learned to understand her too late. "We are more alike than we are different," a wise man once said.

"I'm so proud of you" were the magic words I longed to hear from my grandma, who said them often.

These two thoughts guided much of my career, though the latter still guides me today, more than a decade since she's passed. I progressively and relentlessly continued this path up the corporate ladder to Global Leader at a Fortune 50 company. I did this regardless of, or maybe even despite, being a woman in technology, following the next biggest thing, and chasing the answers to questions like "Where do you see yourself in three to five years?" (The answer to the interviewer is always supposed to be, of course, "your job.")

I decided the potential layoff was a blessing disguised as a curse, and I could craft my future around my purpose precisely as I wanted it. I had time. I was still waiting for those paths on the other side of the fork, or the acquisition, to reveal themselves to me.

I hosted Coach K's workshop in the summer of 2022, and by the fall, I serendipitously met Sulit Press founder and publisher Michelle Savage at a nonprofit annual board retreat. I chased that gut feeling again, leading to my writing in her first multi-author book, where we explored and wrote about "success" and the bumpy roads that led there.

As I explored what to do with my life, I was hopeful the coaching she offered would help me focus my thoughts and point me in the right direction to apply my purpose to my career and life—all on a deadline!

From the first call, the authors silently and collectively decided to bare our souls with one another. We dug deep into the challenges that shaped us and shared them vulnerably. I shared with my new fellow authors, strangers I met for the very first time on this call, stories of my childhood, stories of loss, abandonment, and poverty, of recovery, and of "success." They each, in turn, shared more and more about their stories and challenges from their lives. It shaped our book to become an inspirational reclamation of power as we showed the readers our challenges or "bumpy roads" to our biggest wins.

There were stories of death, tragedy, heartbreak, betrayal, homelessness, divorce, job loss, and other traumas and challenges. Through this process of writing and sharing, a fledgling band of sisters began to form.

Twelve weeks later, in April 2023, the book, a compilation of heartbreaking accounts and comeback stories, became a best-seller!

"Success" had always looked a certain way to me—keep climbing that ladder. Writing in that book taught me that success looks different to different people. Sometimes, it can be a powerful position at a big company; sometimes, it's the success of raising good kids; other times, it can be just putting on pants and getting out of bed after losing someone you love. "Success" is relative.

I was pleased I had written for the book, but the more considerable value was the clarity I received through the coaching process as I reflected on my main issue: using my purpose to guide my career. I still didn't know exactly what it would be, but I knew this was an essential piece in the puzzle, and I was still open to all of the possibilities it might bring.

After the book launch, I met with some of the authors at a networking luncheon for women business owners. I loved meeting those women and I knew I needed to become a member. The women's nonprofit had a position open on their board that would also fill a gap on my resume, and I was interested.

I came home to share the news with my husband about my intent to pay to become a member and how I planned to apply to this role—yet another to add to my long list of responsibilities. He was encouraging, but he challenged me and said it was time I considered starting my own business.

"Start small," he recommended. "At least make enough money to cover the book and the membership. Start there."

My husband planted a seed on my quest for purpose, even if I didn't fully act on it at the moment. That was the next piece of the puzzle of my future that had been missing, and that day, I started brainstorming business ideas and names.

Writing in *Show Your Work* with these women entrepreneurs helped me see more possibilities of what I could do outside of the corporate world. These women had built their businesses and followed their dreams, and I knew I could do the same. If I was going to lose my job, I already had a group of women I could count on to be there as my advisors and friends.

Autumn moved quickly as work increased, and we got closer and closer to this unknown acquisition. I wrote a chapter in another best-selling multi-author book —*Going Places: Soul-Stirring Essays About the Travel That Changed Us*. In September, I took my ERG leaders on what would likely be our last trip together, this time to the Out and Equal Summit at Walt Disney World in Florida, where we were up for their top award! I was also overjoyed to have been selected as a speaker for two larger sessions in front of audiences of about 500 people each. Lines of people formed after each session, full of connections and words of affirmation.

I also had the opportunity to spend a lot of time there with Coach K, who was also speaking at this conference. We talked about personal and professional pursuits, including my new purpose-based business ideas, which I was brainstorming. Our friendship blossomed.

The deep uncertainty at work continued through the fall and increased weekly as we approached the anticipated close date of October 30, 2023. The most anxious week was when people started to get offers from the acquiring company. They were eager to share their excitement on our world chat in Slack, *their* anxieties relieved. I had already decided I wanted to focus on my business ideas after the acquisition. I wasn't sure if I would accept an offer if I received one, yet I still found myself in an unusually anxious week of "will they, won't they?" as my husband and I both awaited offer letters.

We watched nervously as others across the company kept receiving offers, and it felt a lot like the stories you hear of the kid who wasn't picked for the sports team.

Then, the actual acquisition was delayed again, now for a third time, and wouldn't close yet again for a few more weeks. We felt very much in limbo. Some people knew they would continue with the company, and the others, including me, still waited.

I did my best to support my ERG and team members while trying mightily, and sometimes failing, to regulate my own nervous system through the upcoming holiday season.

After almost eighteen months, in mid-November, in the final weeks of waiting for an offer or a termination letter from the acquiring company, I was hit with the unbelievable blow of losing Travis.

Five days after he passed, the long-awaited acquisition closed the day before Thanksgiving 2023. We wondered if layoff letters would come on Thanksgiving Day or if they had the decency to wait.

Travis's funeral service was the Monday after Thanksgiving, another five days after the acquisition closed, yet somehow, no news of layoffs happened over the holiday weekend.

Within a week and a half after my friend had passed away, the acquisition was complete, we celebrated Thanksgiving, and we attended his funeral.

My husband and I drove a couple of hours to the service that morning and arrived early to discuss the show flow with Jina and others who had a role in the service. I did everything I could to make the next hour before the service as smooth for her as possible, finding her water and acting like an attentive event planner. I had been through enough of these.

About ten minutes before the service, I accompanied her to the restroom, where our story began. There, I saw my husband's text from the pews to his family.

After hovering over the email button on my phone, I decided I had to know.

And there it was...my layoff notice. A few deep breaths and thirty seconds later, Jina exited the bathroom. I had to pull it together immediately. Everything about the layoff would have to wait at least a couple of hours, and I needed to be fully present in that moment at his service.

I sang the song how Travis would have wanted it, doing my best to make him proud.

I took time for myself over the holidays, and of course, Travis was on my mind. He had made significant life changes for himself and Jina in the past couple of years— buying a house and moving away, quitting his tech job to follow his dream of running his own catering business, and more. I kept thinking about purpose: my purpose, my career, and how I could use my gifts or strengths to help others. It hit me like a ton of bricks, and with such clarity.

Travis passed away just two weeks after turning fifty. I was thirty-nine with forty on the horizon.

What would he have done if he had been told at forty that he had ten years left? Would he have lived his life any differently?

What would *I* do differently if *I* had only ten years left or less? Would I keep climbing the ladders at software companies, doing what I'm good at but not fully following my purpose? Or would my purpose be better served by using my strengths to help others directly through my work?

It was a no-brainer once I looked at it from this perspective.

On Valentine's Day 2024, I incorporated Soul Purpose LLC. Now, as a business owner and a Clifton-certified Strengths Coach, I train companies and coach people to reach their goals, to follow their purpose, using their natural strengths. This works for individuals and businesses, as once you know and understand your strengths, you can use them to work more effectively with your teammates, your boss, your employees, your stakeholders, and even your customers.

If we could teach people how to regulate their nervous systems, communicate with one another, and love themselves, could you imagine how this world would change?

I now consult companies on how to build better cultures and communities by starting and managing their own Employee Resource Groups. I love speaking about women in business and LGBTQ+ issues. I'm working now on my signature speeches and an eventual TED talk. I have multiple podcast guest opportunities, communities my colleagues and I want to create, potentially my own podcast series, this book, and more business on the horizon. The paths continue to reveal themselves to me, and I am open to exploring where they lead.

As I move through this transition, I know I will still have challenges, but I have my army of rockstar authors and businesswomen who guide me and support me through the changes. My impact will continue to grow as I help others live more purposeful lives, as I'm following my own life's purpose and making this world a better place than where I found it.

Thank you, Coach K, for intentionally sharing your wisdom on purpose and for helping so many, like me, discover ours.

Here's to *living a passionate and purposeful dash*—for all of us.

NATASHA ZIKE

Natasha Zike, PMP is an inspirational trailblazer who brings her strategic and joyful spirit to every endeavor. As an award-winning LGBTQ+ community thought leader, executive leadership consultant, and two-time best-selling author, she leverages over 20 years of global corporate leadership in Fortune 50 technology companies, and beyond, to create thriving business environments. Her communicative, whole-person approach as a diversity advocate and super-connected community creator has made her a sought-after keynote speaker and workshop facilitator.

A Gallup-certified Strengths coach and global Learning & Development specialist, Natasha excels in developing, simplifying, and executing game-changing solutions for her clients. Her soul's purpose is to guide others to live powerfully and purposefully in the face of adversity. Hire this inspirational change-maker for speaking and consulting engagements to transform your team or organization.

www.soulpurposellc.com
www.linkedin.com/in/natashazike/
www.instagram.com/natashazike

*A*ll proceeds from this multi-author book are donated to Central Texas Table of Grace.

Central Texas Table of Grace is a 501(c)(3) non-profit organization that exists to provide emergency shelter services to the foster children and administers our Grace365 Supervised Independent Living program for young adults aging out of foster care. Their support contributes to an improved quality of life for youth and their families. The organization's projects, implemented by an experienced staff, emphasize creating a caring climate for youth. Supporting the development of self-confidence, healthful living, and good judgment, Central Texas Table of Grace provides our children with a thorough foundation for success.

Follow us on social media to find out more.

https://www.facebook.com/centraltexastableofgrace
https://www.instagram.com/ctxtableofgrace/
https://www.linkedin.com/company/central-texas-table-of-grace/
https://twitter.com/CTXTableOfGrace
https://www.tiktok.com/@ctxtableofgrace

Made in the USA
Las Vegas, NV
18 October 2024